Advance Praise for Me 2.0

❝Dan Schawbel's thorough and systematic approach will prove useful to anyone engaged in a job search or looking to find the right career.❞

- **Dipak C. Jain,** Dean, Kellogg School of Management, Northwestern University

❝Read *Me 2.0* and learn the secrets of personal branding from Dan Schawbel, one of the leading voices on the subject!❞

- **Marshall Goldsmith,** bestselling author of *What Got You There Won't Get You There*

❝A great roadmap to create and implement your personal marketing plan in the digital era.❞

- **John A. Quelch,** Lincoln Filene Professor of Business Administration, Senior Associate Dean, Harvard Business School

❝With *Me 2.0* Dan Schawbel has done something remarkable, turning the subtle art of personal branding into a set of systematic and easily implementable strategies for success.❞

- **Robert B. Cialdini,** coauthor, *Yes! 50 Scientifically Proven Ways to be Persuasive*

❝Packed with useful tips, *Me 2.0* can help anyone sharpen his or her personal brand.❞

- **Daniel H. Pink,** bestselling author of *A Whole New Mind* and *The Adventures Of Johnny Bunko*

❝College students, get this book and conquer the new digital recruiting landscape.❞

- **Keith Ferrazzi,** bestselling author of *Never Eat Alone*

❝Schawbel understands the importance of having a strong personal brand when it comes to finding success. This book conveys that wisdom, so rare for a person of his age…so read it or just be plain vanilla in life.❞

- **Tim Sanders,** author, *Saving The World At Work*

❝I wish I had access to a book like this when I was in my 20s.❞

-**David Meerman Scott,** bestselling author of *The New Rules of Marketing & PR and World Wide Rave*

" If you're struggling to find a job or get on the right career path, *Me 2.0* is your solution. **"**

-**Marta Tracy,** *founding producer of E! Entertainment Television and The Style Network*

" At a time when your brand equity is the sum total and composition of your search results, personal branding is everything. If you don't believe me, just type 'Dan Schawbel' into Google. **"**

-**Pete Blackshaw,** EVP, Nielsen Online, and author of *Satisfied Customers Tell Three Friends, Angry Customers Tell 3000*

" *Me 2.0* teaches professionals how to launch their own personal branding campaign using the infinite reach of social media tools. This is an invaluable guide to anyone who wants to achieve career goals in the new Web 2.0 world. **"**

- **Rob McGovern,** CEO of Jobfox and author of *Bring Your 'A' Game: The 10 Career Secrets of the High Achiever*

" Nothing will pay greater dividends than building a personal brand. Not long hours, not hard work, not advanced degrees. Dan Schawbel's four-step plan is a great way to start your own personal branding process. **"**

- **Al Ries,** coauthor, *War in the Boardroom*

" The brand that has the greatest impact on your life is the brand called *You!* Dan Schawbel's *Me 2.0* will show you how to make that brand mean something to others. **"**

- **Bryan Eisenberg,** author of *Waiting For Your Cat to Bark?*

" Amazing…this is a book I'll recommend to every young person I know. **"**

-**Bob Burg,** coauthor of *The Go-Giver* and author of *Endless Referrals*

" People just entering the job market in these very uncertain times need all the help they can get. Dan Schawbel's new book offers tools and ideas that will help guide the next generation down a meaningful path to career success. **"**

-**Stewart D. Friedman,** author, *Total Leadership: Be a Better Leader, Have a Richer Life;* Professor, The Wharton School

"In the fast-paced world of technology, *Me 2.0* pinpoints exactly what you need to do to make yourself stand-out above the rest."

      - **Jon Gordon,** bestselling author of *The Energy Bus and Training Camp*

"... *Me 2.0* is a great resource for all of us, whether we are planning our careers in college or well after graduation. It offers a proven process to find a job doing what you love, which is a secret to success we can all benefit from."

      - **Adrian Gostick,** author of *The Carrot Principle*

"*Me 2.0* shows you how to harness the power of new technology and social media to take charge of your brand and take charge of your career."

      - **Larina Kase,** author of *The Confident Leader and The Confident Speaker*

"If you are looking for your first job, or maybe beginning a new career, do yourself a big favor and read *Me 2.0.*"

      - **John Baldoni,** internationally acclaimed consultant and author, *Lead By Example, 50 Ways Great Leaders Inspire Results*

"Dan Schawbel offers a fascinating look at how to use *Web 2.0* to build a personal brand for professional success."

      - **Randy Street,** author of *Who: The A Method for Hiring*

"*Me 2.0* is must reading for anyone in the 'millennial' generation, but perhaps more importantly for everyone of other generations."

      - **Cali Ressler and Jody Thompson,** coauthors of *Why Work Sucks and How to Fix It*

"Dan Schawbel hits the nail on the head. You must see yourself as a brand to prosper in the new millennium...a necessary message for these turbulent times."

      - **Mark Thompson,** coauthor, *Success Built to Last*

"If you want awesome word of mouth, you need an awesome personal brand. This is the book to teach you how."

      - **Andy Sernovitz,** author, *Word of Mouth Marketing: How Smart Companies Get People Talking*

Me 2.0

BUILD A POWERFUL BRAND TO ACHIEVE CAREER SUCCESS

DAN SCHAWBEL

This publication is designed to provide accurate and authoritative information in regard to the subject matter covered. It is sold with the understanding that the publisher is not engaged in rendering legal, accounting, or other profes¬sional service. If legal advice or other expert assistance is required, the services of a competent professional should be sought.

Published by Kaplan Publishing, a division of Kaplan, Inc.
1 Liberty Plaza, 24th Floor
New York, NY 10006

10 9 8 7 6 5 4 3 2 1

Printed in the United States of America
Library of Congress Cataloging-in-Publication Data
Schwabel, Dan.
Me 2.0 : build a powerful brand to achieve career success / Dan Schwabel.
    p. cm.
Includes bibliographical references.
ISBN-13: 978-1-4277-9820-6

1. Career development. 2. Success in business. 3. Professions--Marketing. I. Title.
HF5381.S285 2009
650.1--dc22
                    2008047878

Kaplan Publishing books are available at special quantity discounts to use for sales promotions, employee premiums, or educational purposes. Please email our Special Sales Department to order or for more information at kaplanpublishing@kaplan.com, or write to Kaplan Publishing, 1 Liberty Plaza, 24th Floor, New York, NY 10006.

This book is dedicated to my grandfather, Max Meenes.

Max is the heart and soul behind my brand. Through the best and worst times, he was a powerful presence who motivated me and pushed me to my limits. No week would be complete without a phone call, when he sat anxiously to hear my status in hopes that one day I would help the world, just like him. As the backbone of my family, Max's love and support will never go unnoticed and will be preserved in memory forever.

Table of Contents

Foreword

by William Arruda

In the Beginning

When I started my personal branding business, Reach, nearly a decade ago, personal branding was something of a novel idea. The concept seemed a little too "Hollywood" to work with "the masses"—at least, that's what one of my colleagues told me when I shared my vision: for Reach to become a global leader in personal branding. To some, personal branding seemed self-indulgent; to others, it seemed frivolous. Yet the process of *personal branding*—unearthing what makes you exceptional and developing plans to use that to demonstrate value and achieve your goals—is of tremendous benefit to any ambitious professional.

The Only Constant Is Change

Today, personal branding is neither novel nor optional for executives and careerists who want to align who they are with what they do and how they do it. According to a 2008 Experience, Inc. survey, 70% of Gen Y employees leave their jobs within the first two years! In the new world of work—where you're only as good as your last assignment or project—your personal brand is the only accepted currency. It's the stability you need in a career that will be filled with change.

The days of the "company man" or woman are long gone. In fact, *change* is the word that best describes the current and future career landscape. The U.S. Department of Labor estimates that people graduating from college in the coming years will have 10 to 14 jobs by age 38(!), and the top 10 in-demand jobs in 2010 will not have even existed in 2004, according to a former U.S. Labor Secretary (Workopolis, 2008[2]). Your personal brand—and reputation—will be the true constant in this ultradynamic environment, where you must constantly demonstrate your value. It will enable you to attract opportunities that align with your skills, passions, and strengths. And it will ensure that you have a career that is both rewarding and successful.

From Obscurity to Ubiquity

Interest in personal branding has grown over the past several years. The term personal branding has become a part of the career industry vernacular, and *career* and *life coaches* around the world have embraced it as the proven strategy for attaining and managing a career.

But it's the rapid growth and popularity of online social networking that has made personal branding accessible and allowed it to seep into all aspects of our lives. Websites like *LinkedIn*, *Facebook*, *MySpace*, and countless others have made personal branding widespread. Personal Googling has become a phenomenon in and of itself, with people Googling each other with astonishing regularity. A study released in 2008 by the Pew Internet & American Life Project stated that Internet users have become significantly more conscious of their digital footprint: in 2007, 47 percent searched for information about themselves online, compared to just 22 percent in 2002[3].

Web 2.0, a term that describes the Internet's new features and applications, including social networking sites, *wikis*, and *blogs*, has greatly enhanced our ability to collaborate and share information. Its inherent community-building and visibility-enhancing features have created the opportunity to establish your personal brand firmly on the Web. Web 2.0 has also made personal branding more tangible and available to people in all stages of their career.

Hiring managers and executive recruiters already routinely use Google and online social networks to evaluate potential candidates. As the hiring process evolves from posting job openings to seeking out ideal candidates, virtual visibility will become more critical to securing the perfect position. This will force all professionals proactively to build their brands online and bolster them in the real world.

Personal Branding as a Corporate Strategy

Personal branding is not just for job seekers. Companies, once reluctant to help their employees build their personal brands, have embraced the concept as a strategy for encouraging leadership and getting the best from their employees. Many of the world's most successful *corporate brands*, including Microsoft, J. P. Morgan, P&G (Proctor & Gamble), and BT (British Telecommunications), have incorporated personal branding into their talent development programs. They recognize their employees' power to deliver on the corporate brand promise in individual ways.

These companies acknowledge that a company succeeds when it demands the *best* from its staff, not the most. And they have learned that employees are more fully engaged when their individuality is unearthed, embraced, and nurtured. The demand for personal branding has increased tremendously and has become the primary focus of my company, Reach. All companies say that their human capital is their greatest asset. The companies who truly believe it have integrated personal branding in their talent development strategies.

The Future Is Personal

Tom Peters' article *The Brand Called You*, which appeared in the August 1997 issue of *Fast Company*, jump-started the personal branding movement. That article was the impetus for my business, and it inspired many others to use the power of personal branding to stand out and deliver professional value authentically. Having been a personal branding pioneer, I have seen many career coaches, executive recruiters, and HR managers join the revolution, but Dan Schawbel stands out among them. His passion for the topic, natural curiosity, and genuine desire to help others succeed have made him one of personal branding's most visible proponents.

Dan wholeheartedly believes in the power of personal branding. He walks the talk, having built an incredibly strong brand of his own through a popular blog, articles, videos, and a magazine. This book distills a lot of his personal branding advice into a comprehensive and thought-provoking instruction manual for success in the new world of work. It provides the "why" *and* the "how-to," and it expresses the urgency with which you need to jump on the "brandwagon."

Personal branding is a celebration of individuality and a burgeoning revolution in the career world. Reading this book is one giant step forward for fulfilling your brand and professional goals.

—William Arruda, founder, Reach Communications
and coauthor of *Career Distinction*

Introduction

The world of work has suddenly changed. Thanks to the meteoric rise of the Internet, traditional methods of communication and career development are evaporating. As a result, businesses of all sizes, from small firms to corporate multinationals, cannot survive by legacy systems alone and will not adapt to these changes without harnessing the power of online technology.

In addition, the Internet itself is changing—evolving into a tool that allows any user to command his future with the click of a mouse. It's no longer just a place to research and discover information; to purchase products; and email your family, friends, or business colleagues. You can connect with people from all over the world, regardless of age, race, gender, religion, and social class, to meet, discuss ideas, and do business.

Amid all of these exciting changes, a new breed of worker is emerging—one who feels energized and empowered by the exciting new world that the Internet has created and is eager to make a difference. Those with confidence, drive, and the ability to use the full potential of modern technology—including creating a powerful personal brand to define themselves and achieve their goals—will be at the forefront of this bold new world.

This book is targeted at college students and young professionals who feel doubt, emotional stress, and fear of failure when approaching the current job market. I firmly believe that this book will help any individual who is determined, hardworking, and excited to realize her personal and professional goals.

The strategies and plan of attack that I have developed and detailed in this book will help you be among these successful individuals. I provide you with *all the tools* necessary to define and achieve your goals. *Me 2.0* describes the history of personal branding; how the Internet has revolutionized career development; and how individuals can leverage social media for personal empowerment, self-management, and networking. It includes a proven four-step process for **discovering**, **creating**, **communicating**, and **maintaining** your personal brand, and it shows you the results you'll achieve by using this plan. It also takes the element of time into account—the sooner you develop your brand, the more prepared you will be for your successful future. *Me 2.0* is divided into three main sections:

- The rise of personal branding
- How to command your career in four steps
- Using your command to achieve success

It also covers my personal branding success story, a framework you can use to achieve similar success, and expert quotes and research to provide you with an even broader perspective on the topic. You'll also get insight into how to use blogs, podcasting, and social networks to put yourself in a position of recruiting power—so that employers will come after *you* for your passion and expertise. Bottom line: This is *your* handbook for surviving and thriving in the digital age—your guidebook for making your personal and career dreams a reality!

- Introduction -

I wrote this book for many reasons. It is mainly the result of my never-ending passion for personal branding and my responsibility to teach others how to protect and promote their own brands. I also saw a real need for a book like this. One thing I've learned after giving lectures on personal branding to global corporations, organizations, and colleges is that most individuals don't understand how to manage their careers in this new Web 2.0 world, nor are they prepared to utilize emerging media to achieve their goals. With this book, my aim is to help individuals unlock the secrets of personal branding, unleash their career potential, and make the world a better place—one brand at a time.

Please refer to *www.personalbrandingbook.com* for additional resources not found in this book.

Part I: The Rise of Personal Branding

Chapter 1

The Brand Called YOU!

No matter who you are, you have undoubtedly purchased products—and therefore *product brands*—from clothing to furniture, technology, and more. As a consumer, you are also personally branded by the various corporate brands you support, whether it be the McDonald's arch on your cheeseburger wrapper, the Nike swoosh on your shoe, or the Apple logo on your iPod. Throughout your life, you have made decisions among competing brands, choosing some brands over others, and along the way you have built up attitudes, impressions, and beliefs—without even noticing.

What does this all mean? As an individual, you must acknowledge that you are a brand. And who better to market your personal brand than *you*. This means that at the end of the day, the success of your personal brand lies in your hands.

The Power of Brand YOU

Personal branding is about unearthing what is true and unique about you and letting everyone know about it. As a brand, you are your own free agent: you have the freedom to create the career path that links your talents and interests with the right position and the ability to move both vertically and horizontally, now and throughout your career. You can even switch career paths when you feel it is necessary.

You also have the opportunity to stand out and make a name—through your brand—for yourself. The fact that owning a website is so easy gives everyone a chance to develop and market a personal brand that shows the world who they are and what they're capable of. For instance, on the Web, you have the opportunity to promote brand YOU by joining a social network and using your page as a billboard to advertise your talents and goals.

Thanks to technology, you can reap the same rewards as the billion-dollar brand names, from Trump to Gucci, through effective *marketing*. Creating a brand isn't just about technology, though. By focusing on delivering results, being remarkable, and learning new skills to adapt to our ever-changing world, you can make your brand memorable, and opportunities for success will follow.

Develop Your Personal Brand

Many people may view personal branding as a form of self-promotion and selfishness. In some ways it is, but this doesn't mean it's a bad thing! Developing your brand makes you a more valuable asset, whether to the company you work for, a potential employer, or your own enterprise. Don't forget, it's your future we're talking about. Don't you want to make it a success? Furthermore, by effectively branding yourself, your career success will translate into happiness outside the workplace as well.

Don't think of the brand called YOU as being confined strictly within a single corporate environment. Even if your current job description and title put you in a corner, both literally and practically, you can—and should—stand out as an individual with a unique set of talents and marketable skills. Remember, no employment contract spans a lifetime, which means you have the mobility and freedom to shape your career path as you see fit.

- If you're on a career path that makes you happy—*work it*. Make the most of your talents and skill set to achieve maximum success.

- If you're on a career path that does not make you happy—*change it*. Find the right path for you and focus on making it work.

- If you're unsure about your future—*define it*. Weigh all the factors that matter to you and find the career path that fits best.

You need to approach your career in terms of *differentiation* (standing out in the crowd) and *marketability* (providing something other people want or need). Why would someone choose your brand?

- A robust professional network
- Endorsements from respected colleagues
- Previous accomplishments with cataloged results
- A diversified and unique skill set

The same rules that apply to corporate brands apply to personal brands. The successful brand YOU marketing model has the proper mix of confidence, passion, likeability, determination, and focus. When you look at successful business leaders, such as Warren Buffet or Rupert Murdoch, you realize that each has a self-purpose, a call to action, and a desire to win. They all shared this marketing model, and you should too.

What Is a Personal Brand?

What is a personal brand? Since *personal branding* is used in public relations, marketing, *entrepreneurship*, social media, and more, many different interpretations of the term have arisen. I was able to solve this confusion by generating a wiki, which is a website that enables collaboration through real-time editing. I then organized a team of global branding experts, including William Arruda, Krishna De, and Mike Myatt, to edit the wiki and develop a definition that accurately summarizes the objectives and goals of personal branding:

If that definition seems confusing, it can be boiled down to this: *how we market ourselves to others.*

> ## What is Personal Branding?
>
> "Personal branding describes the process by which individuals and entrepreneurs differentiate themselves and stand out from a crowd by identifying and articulating their unique *value proposition*, whether professional or personal, and then leverage it across platforms with a consistent message and image to achieve a specific goal. In this way, individuals can enhance their recognition as experts in their field, establish reputation and *credibility*, advance their careers, and build self-confidence."

What It Means to Be You Inc.

We need to keep certain unspoken guidelines in mind when creating *You Inc.* Successful personal brands need to be authentic, have a good reputation, and be discovered by the right people.

Authenticity Is Required

Why do you need to be real? Because everyone else is taken and replicas don't sell for as much! To be a brand means to be authentic. Marketing spin is counterproductive; people filter it out of their minds and send it into a black hole, never to return. If you are presenting yourself as a marketing manager for a *Fortune* 500 company when you are really a cocktail waitress at a nightclub, you obviously aren't legit.

You will notice that many individuals who label themselves as "experts" or "world-recognized" professionals are exaggerating.

Those who pretend to be someone they are not run the risk of being exposed. Just as good romantic relationships are based on genuineness, openness, and a willingness to be up front from the start, in business, your relationships depend on *authenticity*. Authenticity showcases exactly who you are and what you can deliver. For example, if you brand yourself as a freelance writer, you should be able to back that up with a portfolio of solid writing samples.

There is a misconception that branding is all about changing who you are in order to to fit others' expectations. While *image management* is typically just that—a product of conscious manipulation—personal branding is about sincerity.

Beware of False Brand Images

A false image may get you some short-term success, but over time, others will likely see through you—or a formal background check as part of a hiring process will catch you.

Being authentic also includes maintaining open communication and assuming accountability for your actions. Dishonesty will attract more attention than honesty, and the truth always comes out eventually. Rather than constructing a false image and working hard to maintain a deception, you should pay attention to what is truthful and amazing about you and work hard to make the most of it.

A company fails to maintain authenticity when it uses false *advertising* or when its sales force persuades prospective customers to purchase a product they won't enjoy. Would you trust someone who sells you an ugly jacket by telling you that you look gorgeous in it? Each salesperson needs to carry an accurate and truthful message, because that sales rep's customer interactions are a reflection of the corporate brand. Any malpractice must be cleared up and the proper spokesperson should apologize immediately. As your own best salesperson, you need to represent brand *You* authentically.

" Above all else, be yourself—be genuine—and you'll find success no matter what you do. "

—Chris Pirillo, Internet personality
and founder of Gnomedex

To be authentic is to be *transparent*—online as well as in person. Online deceptions are just waiting to be discovered. Thanks, Google!

Here are some examples of brands that maintain a positive online authenticity:

- **Redfin:** Glenn Kelman, known as the "see-through CEO," set up a blog, where he posted about the nasty politics and bad practices conducted in the real estate business (*Wired Magazine*, 2007)[6]. He publicized Redfin's internal debates and arguments about its website design. He even spoke about how he was at a college campus and not a single student went up to network with him. As a result of the blog, Redfin was closing many more deals a day, despite the comments section, where old-school agents fought back harshly.

- **Southwest Airlines:** Southwest started a coauthored blog by 30 employees from the top down to the bottom of the corporate ladder, with conversations relating to work life.

- **Zappos:** This company has a companywide wiki that acts as a feedback loop between employees and management to get problems resolved.

You need to represent yourself accurately at all times. Just like a corporation, if you don't take ownership of your brand, you'll be stuck forever with how the world initially judges you. To have a successful career and save yourself the agony of harsh judgment, make transparency and authenticity an important concern.

Your Brand Reputation Can Make or Break You

Why do you think customers purchase from certain corporations over others? Why do companies spend the largest portion of their marketing budget on branding? Customers purchase based on trust and are willing to pay more for a product and brand they are comfortable with. Effective branding creates customer loyalty, even evangelism. Companies that maintain reputable brands are more successful in gaining and keeping customer attention.

So what does this mean for you as you think about ways to develop your personal brand? As a brand, you can achieve a positive reputation, much like the reputations of companies you admire. Beyond garnering customer attention and loyalty, a major benefit of maintaining a reputable brand—either individually or corporately—is that people will be much more willing to forgive a historically trustworthy company if it fails to meet a specific expectation, such as fast service, provided it show efforts to fix the problem.

In contrast, when a company has a long history of poor service and there is yet another problem, customers will be likely to seek better treatment from a competitor—and there are always lots of competitors eager for the business. Your brand reputation should operate in the same way—building credibility and showcasing your character, attitudes, and actions in ways that instill good feelings in others.

It is your responsibility to put your brand in a favorable light without engaging in excessive promotion. Too much self-promotion, whether among friends, colleagues, or potential contacts, can make you come off as egotistical or self-superior and have a disastrous effect on your brand. Your trail of self-promotion will leave behind a dark cloud that is visible to all. For example, an excessive self-promoter who constantly reminds coworkers of personal achievements in a desperate search for attention and gratification actually alienates potential colleagues and allies.

In attempting to brand yourself within an existing corporation, coming off as obnoxious and annoying will only result in repelling others and may make it more likely they'll either throw you under the bus if a problem arises or try to avoid working with you as projects come up. The workplace is a habitat where the fittest thrive, not by ruthlessly claiming superiority at every opportunity but by strategically positioning themselves as natural leaders. That being said, you can't sit back and watch others take what you deserve. You have to strike a balance to gain the visibility needed to rise to the top.

Making sure your brand reputation is seen as current is also important. When a brand doesn't seem relevant anymore and has no differentiating qualities that make it special, its reputation suffers. People will notice that you seem out of date and avoid your brand. You must ensure that your personal brand stays current, yet it must be consistent over time as well. For example, if you walk into a McDonald's, whether you are in Japan or in the United States, the product you purchase will be consistent, despite small cultural differences. Your brand must strike a careful balance between keeping up with the times and maintaining a consistency that your *audience* can count on.

Brand YOU—Only as Powerful as You Make It

The Power of Word-of-Mouth Marketing

When promoting your brand, *word-of-mouth (WOM)* marketing reigns supreme, as your most important contacts are your friends, family, business partners, and acquaintances. WOM marketing is how to get people talking about you, your product, or your business. Typically, businesses succeed or fail based on referrals, and WOM is a proven way to gain more exposure and build trust fast. In today's increasingly connected world, people become famous, or infamous, because of WOM.

Take Judson Laipply, who showcased his performance *Evolution of Dance* on *YouTube*. The video quickly skyrocketed to the front page of *YouTube* and was featured on countless blogs, social networks, and media sites. This viral effect allowed the video eventually to become the second-most viewed video on YouTube (of all time) with over 100 million views. How much did Judson spend on this campaign? $0. People were so entertained that they shared it with their friends, who shared it with their friends, and so on.

According to a recent study by the Keller Fay Group, 92 percent of people make product decisions based on WOM recommendations[7]. When it comes to personal branding, you are the chief marketing officer for brand YOU, but what others say about your brand often has a greater impact than what you say about yourself. So every time someone talks about you, make sure what they're saying is positive and factual!

Managing your personal brand effectively is essential to controlling word of mouth. The public nature of the Internet has revealed poorly managed personal brands.

- **Exhibit A:** A bank intern faked a "family emergency" to take a day off from work, then dressed up as a fairy for a Halloween party and posted pictures on Facebook the following day (Valleywag, 2007)[8]. The incriminating photo was discovered on Facebook by the manager and passed around the office. The intern lost his position soon after.

- **Exhibit B:** A 20-year-old student uploaded pictures of himself dressed up in a jailbird outfit, celebrating a drinking and driving accident where he injured an innocent woman, onto Facebook (AP, 2008)[9]. Those pictures were found and used in court by the prosecution to convict him—he was sentenced to two years in prison.

You wouldn't want to end up like these two would you?

Visibility Creates Opportunities

A key part of branding is visibility—clearly displaying your value to the world. The more people who either know you or have heard about you, the better. Opportunities for advancement and success will arise through your connections and visibility—created through the repetition and strategic placement of brand messaging. Effective brand messaging allows you to maximize your potential to create positive opportunities.

Brand visibility and awareness are the first steps toward its acceptance by customers. Becoming aware of a brand is the first step in a customer's purchasing process. If people don't know about you, your brand will go unnoticed. Instead of hiding under your bed sheets, push them back and let people know you exist! Visibility allows you to spread your influence. This book will teach you strategies for communicating your brand, but the main idea is that if you want your brand to be known, you have to make it known.

The Power of Brand Visibility

Tim Ferris, author of the number one *New York Times* best-selling book *The 4-Hour Workweek* was virtually unknown to the world before his book was published. He ties his success directly to the relationships he built with influential bloggers and the journalists who wrote about his book when it came out. As each article was published, Tim gained more visibility, which resulted in new and exciting opportunities for him to gain even more personal awareness. This snowball effect placed his book on countless best seller lists, and he was written up in *Maxim*, *Fortune*, and *Wired*; discussed on CNBC; and the list goes on. With a single idea, Tim was able to promote his brand and become a business celebrity, and so can you.

Within an organization, the greatest opportunity for you to gain visibility is through *spheres of influence*. Your "sphere of influence is an imaginary area between you and the individuals who have endorsed your personal brand. The goal of a sphere of influence is to capture the minds of as many of your colleagues or peers as possible and to convince them of your abilities, while establishing trust and mutual respect in the process.

Always Be Networking

To expand your sphere, you must network effectively. The more people who come into your sphere, the greater your chance of success. Furthermore, the object is to get *influential* people into your sphere—they already have large spheres of influence, which you share if you have good relationships with them. With a strong sphere, you can persuade an audience to support you on a project or encourage a recruiter to hire you. As your sphere continues to grow, over time it will turn into a powerful network that can further your career and even open unexpected doors.

How should you go about expanding your sphere? Find ways to interact with your fellow employees and network with as many influential people as possible across groups, departments, and corporate hierarchies. *Networking* occurs in every situation you encounter with friends, colleagues, family, and even teachers. As you befriend others, they will be more inclined to become part of your social life and extend opportunities, possibly in their own corporations.

Don't forget to network outside of your company as well, because there is no such thing as job security anymore. Most people network only when they are searching for a job. When this happens, your intentions are obvious, and people won't go out of their way for you. Be sure to indicate what you're interested in, so when people hear of a job, your name comes to mind. Make your life one giant networking event!

How to Network Successfully:

- Make a strong and favorable first impression.

- Try to remember at least three facts about each person you meet, including the person's name.

- Be conscious of people's feelings when talking.

- Find creative ways to give value or promote other individuals, and they will reciprocate.

- Be an active listener and take a genuine interest in what others have to say.

How Not to Network:

- Interrupt a conversation and force your way into it.

- Ask for an internship or job without even introducing yourself.

- Fail to make proper eye contact or give a firm handshake when first meeting someone.

- Get drunk at an event and spill your beer on the person you are trying to connect with.

- Wear a low-cut skirt, tank top, or other inappropriate clothing to a formal meeting, event, or interview.

- Treat a new contact like a one-night stand instead of forming a relationship.

- Forget your business cards at home, thinking the other person will remember your name and contact information.

- Say you're too busy to help someone else, yet ask that person to support you, and forget to follow up because you're too busy.

- Position yourself as superior to your manager or coworkers.

- Have poor posture and no confidence.

As you seek to rise in an organization, in order to further establish yourself, you must form relationships with others who are already well established. How? You must convince others that you have what it takes and display your intelligence and communication skills by *showing*, not telling.

Here are four rules for climbing the corporate ladder:

1: **Strategize.** Always try to connect yourself with high-profile projects that align with your strengths.

2: **Be efficient.** Finish projects before deadlines and always give recognition to the team when presenting your results.

3: **Productivity is key.** Focus on productivity instead of the length of time you spend on a project.

4: **Promote yourself.** Make sure influential people are aware of your best work, or you risk falling off the radar.

Be a Great Project Manager

In the world of work, demonstrating solid project management skills has become the dominant force in supercharging your personal brand and establishing your reputation—it also looks great on your resume. In the workplace, a project is assigned to you with, hopefully, a specific deadline and the resources necessary for successful completion. Managing the project enables you to produce a measurable outcome, either positive or negative. It also gives you the chance to network with your peers and even across the organization, depending on the scope of the project. Finishing a project successfully creates positive momentum you can build on and a positive reputation. Your track record with projects will convince others that you can achieve the same or better results with the next project.

I learned about the importance of effective project management during college. My first full-time marketing job was with a small product promotion and incentive travel company. One day, I noticed that a colleague was working on a promotional brochure. I showed interest in the project and delivered great results, demonstrating that I had the skills to take her brochures to the next level. Positive WOM about my abilities followed, and soon I was drafting brochures for companies such as WBZ Radio and The Ninety Nine restaurants. More employees quickly started taking notice, and before long, the CEO offered me a full-time position. This success also gave me the confidence I needed to pursue more work of this type. Taking on that project helped me focus and build my personal brand.

Perception Is Reality

Let's say that one day you were sitting outside, having a barbeque with your family, and you observed a snake on the ground. Your first reaction might be to run away screaming, and your behavior would likely cause your family to follow suit. But maybe you all ran away for nothing. Maybe the snake was nonpoisonous and harmless. However, most people connect snakes with poisonous bites on a gut level, regardless of the reality. This simple case highlights the power of *perception*, a quick and intuitive process based on sensations.

Companies are constantly evaluated by the way they are perceived by the competition, their customers, and in the media. If you worked for Enron when its financial scandal was headline news, then your brand was negatively impacted by the misconduct of your company, regardless of whether or not you were personally involved.

Individuals are judged based on perceptions as well. For example, if you come to work wearing jeans in a conservative corporate environment, people may view you as not taking your job seriously, whereas if you "dress for success," people will likely view you positively. On the Web, it is likewise easy to control these opinions and perceptions. By customizing your website to suit the brand perception you want to create, for example, you can influence public perception.

> " Brand is everything, and perceptions are 90 percent of a brand. "
>
> —Paul Kedrosky, analyst, CNBC Television

Think about the power of perception: if you are unhappy with a specific service or product, then you blame the company, right? Every employee selling a product or providing a service is a representative of the corporate brand, so if the employee's brand is perceived as poor, the company will suffer the same effect. In short, in many ways, the employee *is* the brand.

Aesthetics plays a key role in brand perception. Here are two everyday examples:

1: **Hotel bathrooms.** When I go to a hotel or restaurant, I tend to judge the entire place based on my perception of the bathroom. In my opinion, if the business invests in a luxurious bathroom, the entire venue will echo that commitment to quality and service.

2: **Restaurant parking lots.** I evaluate the quality and popularity of a restaurant based on the number of cars in its parking lot. The more cars, the more endorsements the restaurant has.

The point is, in personal branding and in life, little things matter! Each move you make is a chance for you to enhance how people perceive you and draw more people to your brand. Start by wearing professional clothing; having a positive attitude; and conveying a sense of trust, competence, and assurance with each person you meet and interact with.

Those with sluggish, passive, and unimaginative brands will not succeed if they try to communicate an energetic, creative, and dynamic brand to the world. Whether you are a CEO or a junior in high school, you can always evolve your brand. A prime example of brand modification is Madonna. As the years pass and she releases new albums, she repositions her brand to fit the times, using new music technology to remain current. Madonna may have professional image management advisors to coach her, but that doesn't mean you can't follow her successful lead.

Technology and Brand YOU

The World Was Not Ready in 1997

The graduating class of 1997 encountered many uncertainties when they ventured into the postcollege "working world." They had received little preparation for its challenges. Back then, teachers, family members, and guidance counselors made fewer recommendations that students get internships. Job opportunities were growing at a rate of 27.5 percent, the largest increase in history. There were also fewer bachelor's degrees granted between 1997 and 2000 (Scheetz, 1997-1998)[11]. Thus, the need to brand oneself as anything special seemed less urgent.

> Back in 1997 when Tom Peters coined the phrase *Brand You*, he introduced a new idea—that ordinary people could become brands much like Michael Jordan or Tiger Woods. Flash forward to today. As publishing democratizes and flourishes, the media landscape has fragmented into millions of micro niches.

—Steve Rubel, senior vice president, Edelman

When Tom Peters's visionary article, introducing personal branding to the masses, hit newsstands, many individuals weren't prepared, nor did they recognize the potential for using personal branding in their own lives. Instead of pursuing entrepreneurship, the majority sought cover by enlisting as corporate employees and trudged their way up the corporate ladder, because they were instructed to by parents, peers, and teachers. Entrepreneurs at this time connected and recruited primarily through offline means, often through networking events in their communities. Few people thought of using the Internet to bond with investors or join other entrepreneurs and partners through online communities.

Back then, a resume and a cover letter were the sole criteria for the job application screening process, and *human resource* departments collected thousands of them in their database systems. Candidates who appeared qualified on paper were granted standard interviews; hiring managers had only a resume, cover letter, and a standard interview at their disposal. It was challenging for candidates to express themselves freely, showcase their full range of talents, and stand out from the crowd.

" In the past, people played limited economic roles. As employees, they worked within organizational silos where the boss told them what to do. Too many people were bypassed by circulation of knowledge, power, and capital, and thus participated at the economy's margins. "

—Don Tapscott, bestselling author, *Wikinomics*

In the 1990s, the Internet existed in *Web 1.0* format—which meant stationary Web pages with little interactivity. Blogs, which are essentially online diaries written in chronological format, were neither mainstream nor user-friendly, and few people had the technical know-how to run them. Companies preached to users online without actively engaging in the conversations that could lead to positive outcomes, such as the ability to cocreate new products and services.

The costs associated with online branding were sky-high, from developing and designing a website to advertising. Few individuals could afford to brand themselves online for the same price big companies were paying. Media relations were too expensive for most individuals to invest in, and the likelihood they would garner significant attention was minimal. Thus, people were forced to rely on traditional communication channels, including newspapers and print magazines, which provided great circulation at the time but were and are one-dimensional, allowing for little or no interaction.

Like Web 1.0, *Me1.0* was when people hid behind their corporate brand, using their corporate logo as a shield from the outside world. Individuals conformed to corporate policy and had few networking tools at their disposal, so the opportunities for most individuals to broaden and control their careers were limited. There were routine networking events for associations and industries, but there was no mention of connecting through the Internet. The typical career during this time tended to involve long periods of employment at a single company. This "personal brand chokehold" impeded employees, leaving them with few opportunities and one potential income source. Luckily, as time passed, individuals were ready to embrace the fine art of personal branding.

As the corporate landscape progressed to the new millennium, companies started to shift their focus from viewing their talent as "fixed assets" to acknowledging the quality and performance of each employee. People became a corporation's greatest resource and most important product, and the expense of keeping them well trained was viewed as a solid investment (BNET, 2001)[13].

A New Century, a New State of Mind

Enter the 21st century and a new way of thinking, living, and planning for the future. The recruiting landscape has been completely reshaped. Almost two-thirds of the American population—around 194 million people—is online, where the majority of recruiting is now conducted (eMarketer, 2008)[14]. The competition to get jobs is intense; more than 1.5 million graduates will be receiving their bachelor's or master's degrees this year and entering the job market, when the job growth rate is expected to be its lowest in five years (CSM, 2008)[15].

What else has changed? Human resource and hiring professionals now prioritize college major, interview skills, and demonstration of initiative as main factors when deciding whom to hire (collegegrad.com, 2008)[16]. They've also de-emphasized one's GPA in the selection process. Compensation is now a key focus area for employers, given that 56 percent of companies expect to increase salaries and compensation packages to attract, motivate, and retain strong performers (careerbuilder.com, 2007)[17].

> **It's frustrating because I know I could do great work for any company, but it's hard to get that message across when I'm competing against so many other qualified candidates. How am I supposed to stand out? I don't want just any job—I want a great start to a great career.**

—Corey Merrill, graduating senior, Northwestern University

As a result of increasing competition, a large percentage of recent college graduates are still searching for a job. A recent Jobweb.com survey indicated that employers receive an average of 73 applications for each available entry-level position (Monster TRAK, 2007)[18]. Talk about being a needle in a haystack!

This intense competition for jobs is a driving factor in the acceptance of the personal branding practice. Another is the shift to Web 2.0, the transition from one-way communication to community-driven environments on the Web. Out of Web 2.0, *social media* was born.

This new form of media—different from traditional media outlets such as newspapers, television, books, radio, and magazines—is built on community participation. Now anyone can provide remarks on current events or formulate their own stories and receive comments from others.

The *New York Times* and *USA Today* have even implemented reader commentary as a standard application throughout their online articles. They've also borrowed the same sharing features that blogs have, such as *Digg* and *Del.icio.us*, which allow the news to be spread easily from user to user and lets users interact with various websites. You know that media has changed when 95 percent of the top 100 U.S. newspapers and 58 percent of the top 100 magazines offer blogs, and these numbers will surely grow in the next few years (eMarketer, 2008)[19].

The Power of RSS

RSS, which stands for Really Simple Syndication, has quickly become the backbone of how people receive their information online. RSS allows users to view content (feeds) from several websites in one central location. No longer do individuals have to visit many websites to read content. With RSS, people can subscribe to sites and have that content delivered to them. It's like having all the news you need find you, instead of you having to find it.

By 2001, the individual's role on the Internet had shifted from spectator to participant. (Wikipedia)[20]. Like Web 2.0, *Me 2.0* can stand in front of your brand and be an effective brand spokesperson. Blogging was finally adopted by the masses and regarded as a full-fledged phenomenon. Open conversations have replaced one-way dialog on a level playing field. To give you a snapshot, in 2007, there were more than 70 million blogs in the blogosphere (the entire body of blogs on the Internet), as tracked by David Sifry, founder of Technorati. Every day, approximately 120,000 new blogs are developed, with 1.5 million new posts each day worldwide. There is literally a new post created almost every second. Just think about it—every time you blink your eye, a new blog post is published! By 2012, 67 percent of the Internet population will be reading blogs at least once a month (eMarketer, 2008)[22].

As blogs have taken off, *podcasting* has exploded in popularity. Podcasts make multimedia portable, production easy, and sharing seamless, and they have revolutionized the way in which we consume, promote, and distribute information. They also offer an entirely new system for building brand *You*. Now people can be watching a podcast of you anywhere in the world, even without a laptop or desktop computer. You can use a podcast to showcase your talents, such as a video of you speaking at an event, a music video you made with your rock band, or a promotion for your next big business idea. Podcast viewers can get a quick sense of who you are and what you're capable of in just a few minutes. Think of the Web as a giant consortium of talent agents, waiting and watching, trying to find the next big superstar. That superstar can be you!

> **Today's tools make it easier to create, manage, and manipulate a personal brand—and society has realized the value of strong, personal brands.**
>
> —Frank Gruber Sr., product manager, AOL

To sum it all up, personal branding is an amazing and versatile tool and is necessary in a world where technology is changing the way we manage our careers, express our value, and communicate with one another. Personal branding will grant you real meaning and opportunities for success in your life. I've seen many individuals embrace their own passion, in the workplace and socially, through the power of personal branding. They are excited to wake up each day with the confidence to live the life they always wanted to live—and that is exactly how I want you to feel. Personal branding is the ultimate Gen Y career catalyst. It will allow you to achieve your long-term goals in the short term and empower you to become the *commander* of your career.

Chapter 2

Millennials Enter the Workforce

Generation Y (born 1982–2001, give or take a few years) is comprised of over 75 million eager and dynamic young people, and I am proud to say I am one of them (WSJ, 2008)[23]. As a group, we are spearheading the evolution of the workplace, armed with new technology and a new mind-set. As *baby boomers* retire and *Generation X* employees climb the corporate ladder, employers are being held accountable for recruiting and retaining individuals from our age group.

The Gen Y Workforce

Here are some general characteristics of Gen Y workers that sometimes go unnoticed but are worth mentioning:

- We are high-energy and aren't willing to wait an excessive period of time for career advancement opportunities.
- We value our time and want to spend it in meaningful ways, which is why we aren't always ecstatic about accepting entry-level jobs.
- We challenge the status quo because when we were growing up, we were exposed to diverse points of view and many possibilities.

- We know we have many career options, so we are focused on selecting the appropriate one that connects with our passions.

- We readily embrace new technology and use it as our primary form of communication and collaboration, from text messages and instant messaging to whatever comes next.

- We are multitasking superstars: just watch us handle an important cell phone conversation while playing sports!

- We know that results are more important than *appearance*: we'd rather wear jeans and a T-shirt to work instead of a business suit.

" Gen Y are seen as the 'ID' generation, standing for the entitlement 'I Deserve.' They are seen as not being good employees because they are not reliable and that they are not going to be loyal to any employer. Gen Ys must be able to sell their strengths as well as *personality traits.* "

—Robin Ryan, author, career coach, and national speaker

Gen Y Demands Workplace Change

As Gen Y continues to enter the workforce and seize the reins, today's office environment will become barely recognizable. The new office will be virtual, allowing people to work remotely from anywhere in the world, holding videoconferences and using discussion forums to communicate. They'll increasingly come to work in casual attire while listening to their iPods, eager to change the traditional command-and-control work environment.

A Sign of the Times?

Many corporations have begun to prioritize flexibility, work-life balance, and a casual environment to appeal to Gen Y, using special promotions and other career advancement techniques to attract and retain valuable employees (Fortune, 2008)[24].

- **Google** permits its employees to spend a percentage of their time working on nonwork-related projects that they are passionate about, like developing their own software programs. During the day, you can shoot pool, do your laundry, play video games, and even bring your dog to your cubicle.

- **eBay** has meditation rooms for employees.

- **KPMG** offers five weeks of vacation to new employees.

- **Microsoft** grants each employee free grocery store delivery.

The Technology Gap: Use It to Your Advantage!

Often a notable technological gap exists between Gen X and Gen Y employees. While Gen X professionals may have established brand names and enough disposable income to pay other experts for services such as blogging, podcasting, and media outreach, Gen Y has the competitive advantage of early education in these technologies. Gen X has had to work hard to keep on top of the current technological revolution, but for Gen Y, rapid technological change is a common and accepted part of life.

Gen Y is ready and willing to embrace new technology. They are quick to experiment with new methods of communication and to find ways to incorporate it into their lives to become more efficient and productive. If you haven't already, you, too, should adopt this mind-set into your life and use it to your advantage! If you are able to brand yourself as tech-savvy in the workplace, you will become the go-to person for everyone's technology needs. I've been very successful at doing just this, and now I capably field such questions as "How do I use a sum formula in Excel?" It has made me an invaluable asset to my team, and this is how you, too, can become more valuable.

With 50 percent of the entire blogosphere dominated by Gen Y (Technocrati, 2008)[25], it is impossible to ignore our technological aptitude. However, this growth brings greater vulnerability. Now, when companies or individuals make mistakes, the risk of mass exposure is exponentially larger. You could text message a few of your coworkers about something stupid that your manager did, and in no time, your entire office might know about it!

The Gen X-Y Relationship: A Two-Way Street

The relationship between Gen X and Gen Y is a two-way street. Gen X has real-world experience and corporate seniority from which the younger generation could certainly benefit, while Gen Y has a level of tech savvy that their older colleagues could utilize. It's pretty obvious that a relationship of mutual respect and support is the best scenario. Gen Y should not forget the value of having a strong network of Gen X *mentors*.

Support. Professional mentors are supporters—through both successes and failures. They help you overcome obstacles and elevate your professional career. These individuals help mold your brand by providing guidance, resources, and positive reinforcement to steer you on the right path. The best mentors I've had were managers who sat down with me to discuss the results of a project and how I could do a better job the next time around. Keep in touch with them throughout your career, because they are the strongest part of your network and will always be there to assist you.

Connection. To expedite the recruitment process, mentors act as bridges. While many applicants spend lots of time applying and interviewing for jobs, a simple connection from your mentor can allow you to cross a bridge instead of having to crawl under it. Depending on the mentor's status at the company, he may be able to open up a new position or recommend you for an existing one.

Transformation. There is another reason why networking is so important—you never know where you will end up and who will be there. It is even possible for you to supersede your mentor and become a bridge for them. The mentoring relationship comes full circle when you are able to give back to your mentor by teaching them something new. As a member of Gen Y, you can use your knowledge of new technology to help your mentor discover new marketing techniques and expand upon their established brand name. Giving back to a mentor can help deepen your relationship and strengthen your network.

Supporters should always be supported. As you rise and become more successful, these are people with whom you should maintain a close relationship. A great (although fictional) example of this is in the HBO show *Entourage*, in which Vince (an up-and-coming actor) takes his brother, Drama, and friends Turtle and Eric to Hollywood with him as he lives the life of a celebrity. In return, his friends become his employees to sustain his career, with Turtle becoming his driver and Eric becoming his manager.

" The quality of the opportunities you get correlates directly to the work you've done building your personal brand. Strong brand builders get great mentors and solid networks, and those tools, in turn, build stronger brands. In a world where there are no more corporate ladders to land on, your brand is the platform your career will stand on. "

—Penelope Trunk, career columnist, *The Boston Globe*

Here's the bottom line: the workplace has changed considerably in the past decade and will continue to change as technology advances and our behaviors adjust. Your best bet is to stay on top of all the changes as they occur and learn to be flexible. Brand yourself as someone who makes the most of each challenge you face and learn how to use change to your advantage. This includes making the most of your relationship with the generation that preceded you into the workforce. By having an appreciation for what older generations bring to the table and by helping them benefit from your energy, enthusiasm, and technical know-how, everyone wins.

Chapter 3

Introducing Commander YOU!

I was once a victim of the recruitment process. As I transitioned from high school to college to the workforce, I lost count of the number of resumes I blindly forwarded to hiring managers. My various job searches were often emotionally draining and dispiriting processes, but I learned from both my failures and successes. It's my goal for you to learn from both my life experiences and your own and take these valuable lessons to heart as you develop the brand that best positions you for success.

Learn to Sell and Market Yourself

" A few years ago, I walked into the first marketing class of my life and grabbed a seat next to the only kid I recognized. I had no idea this guy would be writing a book on business and marketing at the age of 24. Dan and I have been friends for a long time, and the one thing we always said to each other was be yourself. Now he's taking that age-old concept and revolutionizing the business world with it. "

—Tim Hare, student, Berkeley School of Music

As a teenager, I was clueless as to how powerful marketing truly was. A fellow classmate and now my best friend, Tim Hare, had seen several of the websites I had designed and once asked me, "You are a great marketer—Where do you come up with these ideas?" I had never considered my websites marketing, but I decided to do some research on the subject. I quickly became fascinated by the world of new possibilities it opened up for me, and I focused on learning how I could incorporate the powerful tools of marketing into my life.

Toward the end of high school, after I completed an internship as a salesperson whose responsibilities included cold-calling nearby businesses, I realized that there were two sides to marketing: back-end (sales support) and front-end (sales). I really enjoyed the back-end side, which allowed me to use my Web design and development skills and creativity. I decided to take my newfound love of marketing to the next level. Next stop—college.

College: An Exercise in Networking and Effective Personal Branding

I quickly learned that conquering the college admissions process and getting into one's dream school often required a lot of self-promotion and tenacity. For many people, it's their first big opportunity to brand themselves—as the ideal college applicant—and dazzle the college recruiters. Furthermore, having a successful college experience requires you to develop and hone your networking skills, which you'll keep using as you climb the ladder of career fulfillment. Make the most of your college experience and try to develop these tools, because you'll have many more opportunities to promote yourself and create opportunities for success.

In 2002, I started applying to colleges. I was determined to get into Bentley College (now Bentley University) in Waltham, Massachusetts, and nowhere else, even though I did apply to other schools. I built a complete application package—which in many ways resembles a personal marketing kit—that included a personal essay, academic history, list of personal achievements, and recommendation letters to name a few. Since I was a Bentley early decision candidate, I was expecting a letter sometime in March.

I remember the day it came in the mail as if it was only yesterday. I walked up to my front step, unlocked the door, looked in the mailbox, and there it was—the letter from Bentley. I opened the letter carefully, praying that it would be my lucky day, but it wasn't. I had been deferred from the college of my dreams. This event not only lowered my self-esteem, but it steered me away from wanting to enroll in the other six colleges to which I was accepted.

They say what doesn't break you makes you stronger, and in this circumstance, my determination overpowered my melancholy. I decided that I was going to create another opportunity to show the recruiters at Bentley who I was, what I was capable of, and why I would be a real asset to their school. Through effort and more than a little *persistence*, I was able to arrange a personal interview, and I took this opportunity as seriously as possible. I carefully prepared, making sure that when I arrived on Bentley's campus I was ready to wow them. In sum, I created a personal brand, one of a confident and polished student who looked and acted as though he should be taken seriously.

After the interview, weeks went by, and I heard nothing. Then one day in May, I received a phone call from my mother, screaming that I was accepted. On this day, I knew my life would change forever. I had witnessed the power of effective self-branding firsthand and had seen how dramatically it could change my life.

Make the Most of Your College Investment

On my first day at Bentley, I was determined to continue developing my brand and have a real impact on my campus. I started to venture into unknown territory by participating in student-run organizations. I also met a student in my English class named

Nick, with whom I connected through mutual friendships. He quickly became a pivotal friend who invited me to join the newly established Bentley Entrepreneurship Society, as well as the Bentley Investment Club. I also joined the Bentley Marketing Association and was able to increase my marketing savvy, as well as network with some great people—many of whom turned out to be important contacts later on in my life. I also joined a fraternity, Alpha Gamma Pi, and gained lifelong friends and a powerful network of fraternity brothers.

Beyond offering networking opportunities, college is the ideal place to discover and develop your talents and skill set and begin showing the world how you can use these in the world of work. I decided that a career in marketing would make the best use of my ingenuity and aptitude for Web design and writing. I took classes in marketing, business law, team management, economics, and managerial accounting while doing website consulting and collateral design outside of the classroom.

The Power of Internships

Compared to some other fields, the competition for entry-level positions in marketing is intense. A great way to enhance your personal brand and desirability as a potential employee is through internships. I started out using networking as a way to get internships and to create opportunities for *cross-learning*, which means to learn about all related areas of a field. I strongly recommend that you embrace the power of cross-learning. Success in most fields requires you to know things about other, related fields that you'll be involved with. For example, I took the time to learn about public relations, promotions, and direct marketing to round out my marketing skill set.

After a few local internships, I taught myself how to develop a portfolio to use when applying for other internships. It was time to find out if I could claim internships based on my experience rather than my network. My approach throughout this process was driven by my "never give up" mentality and my relentless focus on becoming an outstanding marketing applicant when I graduated.

I strongly recommend that you choose your internships carefully and go after opportunities that will enhance your skill set and desirability to future employers. My next internship was with Lycos, where I was educated in *public relations* and content production. I received no money, but the experience was valuable to my future as a successful marketer. I also learned that if I wanted to be successful tomorrow, I had to sacrifice today.

The Bottom Line

Consider every opportunity a chance to improve and promote your personal brand. Whatever your personal goals are, maintaining this positive attitude will open up pathways for advancement and success in your life!

After Lycos, I wrote a letter to a marketing manager at Reebok, where I had been turned down for an internship several months ago. Just as I did when interviewing at Bentley, I took this opportunity very seriously and worked hard to sell myself as the ideal candidate. I was interviewed twice, and after a few months, I was offered the internship. This was another instance when I proved to myself that if I worked hard and was persistent, I could achieve anything. Of course, I didn't stop there. During the summer of 2005, I interned at both Reebok and LoJack. I wrote a marketing plan for LoJack and assisted Reebok with its fall catalogues, meeting both 50 Cent and Venus Williams in the process!

I noticed that as my internship experience and leadership positions increased, more students sought mentorship from me. While still an undergrad, I became actively involved in helping other students shape their own career paths. By diversifying my experience in marketing through a variety of successful internships, I was ready to confront—and conquer—the senior year recruiting process.

Navigating the Entry-Level Job Maze

It should come as no surprise that college graduates face intense competition for entry-level jobs. As the competition continues to heat up, a successful job candidate has to make a strong case why he is clearly the best person for the position. There's no better foundation for doing this than by having a powerful personal brand with something that makes you stand out from the crowd.

When I decided that I wanted to do product marketing for a large corporation, I entered the recruitment arena in full force. I constructed a set of marketing materials with an associated pitch to show that I was ready to hit the ground running on my first day. I drafted a professional resume that played up my individual strengths and skill set, an effective cover letter, a list of references, as well as an item that would help distinguish me from others—a CD portfolio. I remember telling my parents, "This is it. This is what's going to separate me." I applied to over 40 companies in search of the perfect job that would match my skills, interests, and goals and was located in the greater Boston area.

I identified EMC as my employer of choice. It was located in Massachusetts and, according to friends who had worked there previously, provided superior compensation, benefits, and real-world work experience. It was a challenging process even with my background and credentials; the company's distinguished reputation meant the competition was unyielding.

As I went to a series of interviews, I noticed that hiring managers paid special attention to three items: the personal story that I told, my CD portfolio, and my enthusiasm. My storyline gave the hiring managers an understanding of my personal identity and career strategy as well as my perseverance, which clearly reflected my desire for the position. The portfolio displayed my creativity, uniqueness, and seriousness. And my enthusiasm verified that I would be a dynamic force, ready and eager to be a real asset to the team. After several interviews, which gave me access to many important people in the marketing world, I was selected as a member of the solutions and services team.

> **Dan treated the initial informational meeting as the formal interview—his one chance to communicate his personal brand. Dan's resume, promotional CD, and unwavering eye contact communicated experience, confidence, and tenacity. Dan quickly rose to the top of our list, and soon after, we extended an offer.**
>
> —Joe Markey Sr. Marketing Manager, EMC

My first job out of college was the result of years of careful planning, hard work, and an unyielding focus on achieving my career goals. Your path to success should include the same level of dedication, and your personal brand should clearly reflect your commitment to making your future a success.

Become a Career Commander

Each person, including you, possesses a unique set of qualities and an unlimited reservoir of potential. Unfortunately, most people don't realize this until it's too late. If you're concerned about remaining stagnant throughout your career or living an "average" life, then this book will help you gain the confidence, self-esteem, and focus you need to take control of your future and make it a successful one!

You may not be enlisted in the military with a star emblem on your pointed hat, but you *are* a career commander. With the tools provided in this book, you will no longer feel as through you have to allow yourself to be treated like a peon or a "worker bee." Today is the day you exemplify a commander—an individual who has the confidence, mental strength, stamina, and posture to conquer the recruitment process.

> **"** I kicked off my un-keynote at the first Pod-Camp by telling everyone there that they were superheroes. Why? Because through their use of social media, they had the power to bypass hierarchies, discover and connect to meaningful two-way conversations, and build value and brand without getting permission to do either. **"**

—Chris Brogan, cofounder, PodCamp

Why am I making so many military references? Think about it: a military commander holds accountability for and authority over a group to achieve a common goal. To be a commander is to be a leader, and with the position, you gain the belief that you are in charge. Commanders can conquer anything—including the recruitment process—and be successful within any business environment.

You Have the Power!

Social media has enabled individuals to have as much—or more—presence as large companies:

- **Companies** typically have a single branded website. Each change made to the website often must go through a lengthy approval process.

- **You** can start multiple websites in the course of a day without asking for approval.

- **Companies** rely on PR agencies and advertising budgets to get their names out there.

- **You** can network with people online and be written about on several sites in a given day.

- **Companies** often require spokespeople to talk on behalf of their brand.

- **You** *are* the brand, so you can talk on behalf of yourself.

What Does It Take to Be a Commander?

Being a commander is a state of mind, and by reading this book, you've already taken the first step toward unlocking the commander within you. As the commander of your career, you influence, inspire, and earn respect from others. Your rewards are positive relationships, opportunities for success, and—hopefully—monetary compensation.

Picture the Web as a gigantic rock concert, where everyone has a microphone that can either stay muted or be amplified to reach a broad audience. No longer do you have to hide in the shadow of a corporate brand—it's time to make a name for yourself. Anyone in the world—yes, even you—can establish a brand through blogs, podcasts, social networks, or even standard Web pages and hold your own rock concert. You can grab people's attention with a brand that cannot be ignored and make a real difference!

What It Takes to Be a Career Commander

To be a career commander means...

- to be an active leader in and out of the workplace.

- to learn from mistakes and failures, while never holding grudges and always putting bad experiences behind you.

- to know no bounds and persist against all odds.

- to stand tall and have a memorable presence.

- to be an agent of change who seeks to lead by example.

- to care for others, show respect, and follow the Golden Rule.

- to take pride in yourself and your accomplishments.

- to always give back and support those you cherish most.

The four main qualities of a successful commander are **leadership**, **passion**, **teamwork**, and **confidence**. By concentrating on improving each of these qualities, you will be better prepared for the long road ahead.

- **Leadership** skills let you spread your influence and ideas to others. Leaders are respected figures who can get things done. To accomplish your goals, you need others to support your growth. As a successful leader, your followers will be more inclined to leverage their networks in support of your cause.

- **Passion** comes from within. It is rocket fuel for your personal brand. When you have passion, you never give up, despite the obstacles you will encounter. Passion will enable you to have a positive attitude and mind-set as you set forth in developing a superior brand.

- **Teamwork** is one of the most rewarding and prized attributes of today's corporate environment. Most job descriptions plug "being a team player." For major projects, you will need the combined network and intellect of your coworkers to hit milestones and deliver results.

- **Confidence** is the spine of your personal brand. When you're confident, you don't back down, you gain respect, and you have a great sense of self-being. Whether in the workplace or in your social life, confidence will make you successful.

To be successful as commander YOU, you first need to learn about all the aspects of your personal brand, then you must take action. Don't forget: the only person who can make you successful is *you*. If you take a backseat in your career and let other people command your future, success will pass you by. In this Web 2.0 world, *you* are empowered to accept or reject other people, to define your brand clearly, and to help make the world a better place. It's time to take a stand, put your foot down, and take pride in who you are!

Chapter 4

The Many Aspects of Personal Branding

Don't be uncomfortable being labeled as a "brand." You've already been branded without even realizing it! You are a representative of the products you buy, the lifestyle you live, and the connections you have. You are already brand YOU! Furthermore, in almost every situation, whether you realize it or not, you are "selling" something.

When you're trying to entice your friends to go to a movie or grab a drink at a bar, you're trying to sell an idea. You are using your sales skills and brand leverage to convince others to follow you—and you're being judged based on your approach. Each romantic encounter you have is, with all due respect, a selling proposition—from the first conversation to the moment a relationship is agreed upon, you are working to assure another that he or she is making the right choice.

In organizations, you are often paired with other individuals to work on various projects, and although each member of the group brings opinions and expertise, those with the best sales pitches typically take control of the group. The more you understand the significance of personal branding and its role in your life, the more you will appreciate it and be motivated to discover how you can use it to stand out.

The Octopus Model of Brand Relevancy

As you can see in Figure 4.1, the subject of personal branding, like an octopus, has eight "tentacles," or subtopics. Each tentacle has "suction cups" for sensing and interacting with things around them. Personal branding connects to each related topic in a similar way. Your personal brand is like the head of the octopus, and each tentacle represents a key area that either impacts or is influenced by your brand.

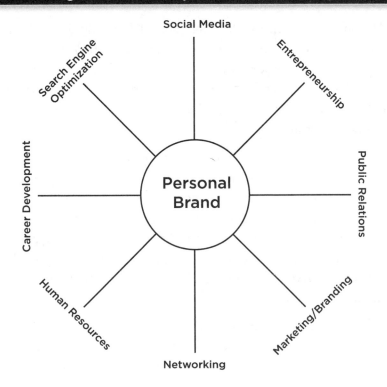

Figure 4.1. The Octopus Model of Relevancy

Marketing/Branding

Marketing is one of the core functions of business. As more and more start-up businesses are launched each day, marketing becomes an integral part of getting your new venture known to your target audience and standing out from the crowd.

The Meaning of Marketing

The American Marketing Association (AMA) updated its definition of marketing in 2007 as follows[26]:

"Marketing is the activity, conducted by organizations and *individuals*, that operates through a set of institutions and processes for creating, communicating, delivering, and exchanging market offerings that have value for customers, clients, marketers, and society at large."

Traditionally, marketing focused solely on a specific business enterprise. In today's society, everyone needs to be a marketer of his or her own brand! Whether you are a student, employee, business owner, or chairperson of the board, you need to recognize the new rules of marketing and how to communicate your message to others appropriately.

The Tools of Marketing

Marketing, by nature, creates a transaction between a buyer and seller, using promotion, advertising, public relations, direct marketing, and other methods to target a select market.

- **Promotions:** A "buy one get one free" coffee deal at Dunkin' Donuts

- **Public relations:** Having a corporate spokesperson quoted in a *New York Times* article

---

> - **Advertising:** A paid placement in the *New York Times*, such as a graphic banner at NYTimes.com
> - **Direct marketing:** An email blast to 5,000 customers, notifying them of a new product release in the coming weeks

Branding is a marketing concept that involves creating an image that resonates with the attitudes, behaviors, and perception of the target market. A brand creates a connection as well as an experience in the minds of other people. A brand conveys a sense of trust, and your favorite brands are like your best friends; they never let you down.

> **A brand is powerful when it stands for a word in the mind of the consumer. It doesn't matter if that brand is a product, a company, or a person—the same laws apply. The key to success is a narrow focus, a good name, and a strong position.**
>
> —Laura Ries, coauthor of
> *The 22 Immutable Laws of Branding*

When watching the Red Sox play or eating at a five-star restaurant, you're paying for a brand experience. An experience sparks an emotional connection—and may entail a premium price. Brands have a reason for existing; they can make you smile, laugh, cry, and more. Each brand carries a set of *values* that are embodied by the product, the corporation as a whole, and the individual employees who support it (be it 1 or 100,000 dedicated people).

There are three types of brands:

    1: Corporate. The name, logo, and personality of any company. Corporate branding refers to using a corporate brand name to promote a product. For instance, Dove places its corporate brand name on bars of soap in hopes that you'll purchase them based on your previous experience with the Dove brand, a commercial promoting it, or one of your friends recommending it.

2: **Product/Service.** From a pen to a guitar to a car, a product is something you can touch. From lawn care to a haircut to legal advice, a service can't be touched but makes your life better nonetheless. A corporate brand exists through products and services that hold its name.

3: **Personal.** Unlike a corporation, you don't need to put your name on a product to sell yourself. A person is a type of product and, like a product, requires marketing. This means that you can adopt several brand strategies in your own life, such as producing a website.

Corporate, product, and personal branding can also mesh in an integrated approach: just ask Donald Trump. The Trump Corporation produces Trump University, Trump Tower, Trump Taj Mahal, Trump Books, and Trump Restaurants. The personal brand is Donald Trump. Notice how all products and the corporate body are *brand extensions* (using a brand name in support of a product in a different category) of Donald Trump, the individual.

As a billionaire brand, Donald is approached by many companies that want to place the Trump name on their product. Why? The Trump "stamp of approval" conveys quality, professionalism, and success. If the product doesn't measure up to this standard, it will not receive the stamp. There's a lot to be learned from this strategy:

- Don't be afraid to reveal your true personality in all that you do. By doing so, you are investing your products and services with your personal brand.

- Put your name on everything you're proud of whenever possible, because then people will remember your personal brand positively.

- Be conscious of what projects carry your name, because their quality is a reflection of you.
- Even strong marketing can't save a personal brand with an image of poor value.

Figure 4.2 highlights some other successful brand extensions—individuals who have successfully extended their personal brands into corporate/product endeavors.

Figure 4.2. Personal Brand Extensions

Personal Brand	Corporate/Product Brands	Feelings and emotions expressed
Jay-Z	Rockefeller Records, 40/40 Club, New Jersey Nets, Rocawear Clothing	Proud, cool, aggressive, and demanding
Sarah Jessica Parker	*Sex and the City* TV show, Sarah Jessica Parker Fragrances, Bitten clothing line	Sexy, tragic, and supportive
Emeril Lagasse	Cookbooks, Food Network TV show, Emeril's Gourmet Produce (grocery products), Emeril's Restaurants, Cookware line	Flamboyant, passionate, and loud
Paris Hilton	Hilton Hotels, Records, The Simple Life TV show, "Just Me" fragrance line, Club Paris nightclubs, Rich Prosecco Champagne	Spoiled, conceited, and dramatic
Paul Newman	"Newman's Own" Food Company, "Newman/Haas/Lanigan Racing" Racing Team	Charitable, honest, and driven
Hugh Hefner	*Playboy* magazine, The Girls Next Door TV show	Confident, romantic, and compassionate

Even fictional characters like Mickey Mouse (Disney) and Ronald McDonald (McDonald's) have personal brands that express their company's brands. These companies use these characters to reach out to individuals on a personal level and to personify their brands. This goes to show that personal branding can be tied to success with product and corporate brands.

Just as a personal brand can express a company brand, a product brand can fortify a company brand name. A good example is the relationship between Microsoft's Xbox and the Halo video game series. As the demand for Halo increased, so did that for the Xbox, bolstering Microsoft's brand. When consumers associate a particular product with a certain corporation, they tend to think of the corporation more positively. On the flip side, when Dell had to recall 4.1 million notebook computer batteries due to a safety risk, the battery recall created a negative perception of the Dell brand.

The Power of Brand Image

Every company, whether a *Fortune* 500 company or a small firm, has a brand image. Companies that manage this image carefully increase their value. You can increase your own brand value by managing your own image, whether in the workplace—by taking the initiative whenever possible, working well with your peers, and finishing projects on time—or in your own venture—by controlling the look and feel of your website, logo, products, and messaging. To be successful, you don't need to become a celebrity or endorse products. You can implement similar branding strategies when looking for a good job, such as using business cards and portfolios to leave a lasting impression.

The table in Figure 4.3, from Interbrand and *BusinessWeek's 100 Best Global Brands 2008* report[24], shows some of the world's largest global brands and the feelings and emotions they try to convey. Although you may never be as large as the corporate goliaths, you, too, can control your brand image, so make it true to yourself and your goals.

Figure 4.3. Global Brand Images		
Brand Name	**Brand Value ($millions) measures financial analysis, brand analysis and brand strength**	**Feelings and emotions expressed**
IBM	66,667	Refreshing, hip, and sporty
Microsoft	59,007	Leadership, history, and novelty
Coca-Cola	59,031	Prestige, strong, and built to last

A great benefit of Web 2.0 is that effective advertising can occur without your having to spend a ton of money on traditional outlets like TV, newspapers, or radio. For example, Google uses word-of-mouth marketing to create a viral buzz throughout the Internet and AdSense (their contextual advertising solution for website owners) to remind people of its existence. Having multiple websites use *AdSense* not only benefits website owners, who want to make money, but Google, whose name you repeatedly see across the Web, who wants to maintain a powerful brand image.

Weezer, a popular rock band, created a video for their "Pork and Beans" single, featuring a handful of Internet superstars, such as Tay Zonday (Chocolate Rain). Although the video was on TV, the viral effect of the Internet spread it to over 14 million online viewers (*Seattle Times*, 2008)[30]. General Mills started a viral campaign called "Pink for the Cure" to spread hopeful stories of those touched by breast cancer. It developed a MySpace page, which was endorsed by celebrities, such as Carson Daily, where breast cancer survivors and activists could share their stories. The result was more than 2.7 million participants (Marketing Sherpa, 2008)[31]!

Public Relations

Companies use PR to keep their image in a positive light or release new products through various media channels. PR agencies charge high fees, because they have already built relationships with the media and have experience pitching and creating press releases. Although you don't need to hire a PR agency to appear in magazines or newspapers, you do have to form relationships with reporters and journalists who cover the topics in which you're interested. You can use PR to get your name out there and establish a line of credibility. When an individual becomes their own PR person or spokesperson, I refer to this as *personal PR*.

Personal PR Strategy–Dos and Don'ts

- **Do:** Read magazines, newspapers, websites, and blogs to find articles that match your interests.

- **Do:** Respond to articles written by journalists, reporters, or bloggers by pointing out parts you enjoyed, as well as giving your opinion, via email. Maintain a consistent dialogue with influential people at each website or blog and gradually introduce your own product or ideas.

- **Do:** Include a custom signature in each email you send, which includes your name, area of expertise, a website or blog URL if you have one, and a preferred method of contact.

- **Don't:** Don't let unanswered emails break your self-esteem; it happens to the best of us. Your best bet is to keep trying until you hit an oil well.

When you start building your brand, few people will know who you are, so it's crucial that you proactively reach out. This is how you start forming key relationships and become noted as a source for specific types of information, products, or services. Unlike advertising, which guarantees a certain placement for a price, PR is an interesting beast, because there is no guarantee you will be headline news.

Here's some advice on how not to respond to the media:

- **Avoid** sending too much email to a single journalist. They may consider it spam.
- **Never** send a press release or pitch without at least introducing yourself first.
- **Don't** write overly aggressive or inflammatory emails or you will turn people off.

Press can be positive, negative, or neutral. Some young celebrities make headlines for drinking and driving or by appearing bald on television after bashing a car with an umbrella, but you should be seeking as much positive press for your brand as possible. Positive press typically occurs when you are quoted as an expert source or when you've accomplished something noteworthy and are written about. When handled properly, the benefits of positive personal PR include increased traffic to your website; increased credibility and exposure; and the ability to leverage your personal brand for new opportunities for success.

Human Resources

Human resource (HR) professionals are often charged with recruiting and retaining employees, overseeing compensation and benefits, and upholding and promoting the corporate culture. One of their goals is to hire the most talented staff at the least possible cost. HR recruiters connect qualified candidates and hiring managers to fill positions. They often do so by pulling resumes from the corporate database, using key words to find candidates that match job descriptions. Many companies also have referral-based systems, where current employees recommend suitable candidates. As technology evolves and the number of job search websites increases, HR's job gets more challenging, and the process of weeding out the poor candidates from the strong ones gets tougher.

HR increasingly writes job descriptions that incorporate personal branding. In 2007, Pew Internet and American Life Project reported that 18 percent of working college graduates said that their employers expected some form of self-marketing online as part of the job[32]. The idea is simple: if you're not visible, you're not found. If employers don't allow their employees to be found, they will suffer, because their competitors will permit employees to brand themselves.

> Until roughly five years ago, finding great talent was like finding a needle in a haystack. Today it's like finding a needle in a stack of needles. Monster contains 44 million resumes. CareerBuilder has 17 million. HotJobs has 5 million. And that's just the tip of the iceberg. Facebook, LinkedIn, Spoke, and numerous other online networks add to the clutter. The amount of noise in the employment marketplace is unbelievable.

—Harry Joiner, executive recruiter, MarketingHeadHunter.com

Recruiting Goes Web 2.0

Personal branding will become the cornerstone of recruitment as the adoption of social media and networks expands, and the competition heightens—both between job seekers looking for positions and employers seeking the best applicants. From screening to interviewing and candidate selection, the recruiting process will be controlled by social media and networks, where recruiters can connect with the right candidate to match their open position and engage in a virtual conversation. According to a report from Classified Intelligence LLC, 61 percent of employers view social networks as a promising channel to discover candidates.

Traditional resumes don't differentiate our brands, as they don't capitalize on our personalities. Social media will put the personality into resumes. The traditional resume will evolve, encompassing more social media components, such as podcasts and sharing mechanisms like Digg. To address the concern of how these multimedia resumes can be read by various technologies, new organizations dedicated to making this process more efficient will appear. Resumes will be shared, critiqued, and consumed within social networks, creating a pathway for the right recruiter to select the right applicant at the exact time a position opens.

Simple online job boards like Monster.com and Careerbuilder.com may dominate the job-listing scene, but the tools of job posting and search are evolving. We are already seeing signs of this transformation:

- **Simply Hired** and **Indeed** aggregate millions of listings from other job and corporate sites, and subscribers receive RSS feeds or email alerts when jobs match their profiles.

- **Jobster** is a social network for job seekers and recruiters, allowing companies to recruit talented contacts and seekers to network with individuals who work at companies of interest.

- **NotchUp** lures talented-but-complacent workers and managers into a recruiting pool, where companies pay to interview you. You can set your price or use NotchUp's calculator to discover the value of your brand, and the site acts as a filter for both the prospective employer and employee.

- **Blogs** have already started hosting their own job boards using **Jobamatic.com**. There are even jobs specifically for blog writers. Job searchers don't have to perform cumbersome searches within large job boards; RSS will actually feed the jobs directly to them.

- We are already seeing **niche websites** catering to specific industries and job functions, including media, real estate, major league sports, accounting, and the food and beverage industry. This trend will continue.

- Emerging tools include **video podcasts** of what it's like to work at a company to Q&A videoconferencing sessions, where current employees can give advice to prospects. Applicants will develop more appealing cover letters and be better prepared for interviews, because they have more corporate information and contact names at their disposal.

- Job seekers will conduct extensive searches on **Google**, **YouTube**, and other sites to learn as much as they can about companies before bothering to submit their resume or connect directly with a hiring manager. They are getting much smarter about how they confront recruitment. Job postings and informational interviews are already exposed in online multimedia formats. **Jobs in Pods** broadcasts phone interviews from employers seeking candidates to fulfill new jobs at such companies as IBM and TJX. Applicants are learning about positions from those who are hiring or who work in the hiring group, so they become knowledgeable before resume submission.

Just like you, everyone wants to feel special and be the one chosen from all the other candidates for a dream position. To accomplish that goal, candidates need to be aware of the latest trends in virtual job boards—before the competition swarms around them.

The New Career Search Toolkit

The reality is that traditional resumes will remain for the time being, due to existing HR database management systems. The good news is that companies as well as applicants now have some new tools in their toolkits. There are several supplements to a traditional resume, including LinkedIn and Facebook profiles, *video resumes*, blogs, and even *virtual worlds*. These tools can reveal an applicant's experience, marketable talents, interpersonal skills, and personality.

A word of caution: Anything negative that exists online can readily be found by a potential employer, often through a simple Google search. In fact, Clearswift confirms that 77 percent of HR managers understand these new tools and browse social networks looking for candidates[34]. So be careful: do your best to ensure that Web content presents you in a positive light.

> **"** I think social media will ultimately change how HR recruits, and it is changing the entire talent marketplace. You are there to be found by your entire network, conceivably for the rest of your lives. That is a profound change. I believe the effect will be less 'applying' for jobs, more of employers finding you. **"**
>
> —Libby Sartain, chief people officer, Yahoo!

LinkedIn

LinkedIn is a professional network with millions of active users. It is also a recruiting database, connecting recruiters with talented users and resumes. Each user profile can be personalized to feature recommendations from colleagues, a self-portrait, relevant links, and special interest groups. This dynamic resource updates automatically as your network expands and evolves.

> **"** Networking has always been important. LinkedIn just made it easier. **"**
>
> —Olya Dadressan, SIS career advisor, American University

LinkedIn fuses a resume, cover letter, and reference document together by having the typical fields you would see on each. For example, you can input your work experience job by job (resume); summarize your qualifications, goals, and interests (cover letter); and gather electronic endorsements from your managers (references document).

With this new technology, HR professionals can search through LinkedIn to find candidates who match available positions, while candidates can freely search their network for career opportunities. Consultants and entrepreneurs use the LinkedIn Answers feature to ask and answer questions, providing valuable expertise that attracts new clients.

Use the following LinkedIn strategies to your career advantage:

- **Craft your profile.** The major sections of your profile are your professional summary; experience; education; recommendations; and additional information, such as your websites, interests, and groups. Make sure you fill out all the sections the best you can and use key words as much as possible, because that is how recruiters will find you.

- **Start and expand your network.** Conduct searches to find people you've met throughout your career or personal life (classmates, coworkers, etc.). After adding a contact on LinkedIn, be sure to find out to whom they are connected so you can eventually expand your network.

- **Control your Google results.** LinkedIn ranks very high in Google, so when you create your account, use your full name. When you Google your name, your profile should show up in the top ten results.

- **Ask for advice.** LinkedIn Answers allows you to ask or answer a question from within your network. It is a great place to receive career-related advice or to help members in your network.

- **Get recommendations.** You can give and receive recommendations from clients, coworkers, managers, and partners. These recommendations act as firsthand endorsements of your performance in a current or past job and are looked on very highly by recruiters.

- **Search jobs.** You can conduct job searches using LinkedIn, and the people in your network might be a potential bridge to a new job opportunity.

Facebook

I was introduced to the power of Facebook during my junior year of college. I remember it like it was just yesterday. My friend came running down the hall saying, "I just got Facebook for our school." Of course, my first question was "What the heck is Facebook?" He explained it to me, and although I and many other friends completely blew it off at first, by midsemester, we decided to enroll and see what the hype was all about. In general, Facebook was a simple and effective social networking tool with very little clutter and the ability to post photos from social events.

One year later, as a senior in college, students all across campus were using it on a daily basis—to communicate with friends, meet new people, and spread the word about various campus events. Since then, it has exploded in size and scope. Facebook was initially branded as a tool for college students to keep in touch, and if you had told me in college that it would be used for connecting with professionals and advancing your career, I would have laughed. I wasn't laughing when my manager Facebooked me though!

A lot has changed since then. Facebook has opened up its platform to the world. They have even allowed users to develop their own applications; there are now thousands of customized *widgets* on different profile pages. Have you been "superpoked" or "bitten by a vampire" yet? Yes, these are just a few of the applications that have been developed.

Professionals often promote their products and companies on Facebook, and recruiters screen Facebook for incriminating photos. Vault recently reported that 44 percent of employers log onto social networks like Facebook to examine the profiles of job candidates, and 39 percent have looked up the profile of a current employee[35]. Even the CIA uses Facebook to recruit potential employees into its National Clandestine Service (*Wired*, 2007)[36]. You can't treat Facebook as just a party anymore! Be mindful of what pictures and information you post.

Use the following Facebook strategies to your career advantage:

- **Control your page.** Go to the privacy section on Facebook and change "Photos tagged of you" to "Only me." Do the same with videos. When you set these privacy preferences, no one will be able to tag you in a picture or video and have it automatically appear on your page without your consent.

- **Complete your profile.** While LinkedIn directly addresses your professional profile, Facebook caters more to your social interests. A Facebook profile isn't complete without your favorite quotes, TV shows, hobbies, music, hometown, and birthday. The more fields you fill out, the more someone can learn about you.

- **Find your contacts.** Aside from searching for your friends, family, and colleagues, you can retrieve friends from your AIM, Gmail, Yahoo!, and Windows Live contacts.

- **Nonstop networking.** The easiest way to network on Facebook is to write, "Happy birthday," on your friend's wall, once Facebook notifies you of the date. Also, you can comment on your friend's status messages, join your company or area network, and speak directly to your friends using the Facebook IM feature.

- **Join groups and fan pages.** Search for special interest groups and try to locate groups in your region, so you can find suitable friends or business contacts. In the same regard, locate pages of public figures or products that you care about and talk with other fans.

- **Register for events.** If you want to meet people like you, then register for events in your area using Facebook. Events list the people who are attending, and it's wise to connect with a few before you attend the event to feel more comfortable.

Blogs

Blogs started off as digital communities and forums and then evolved into online diaries, where people kept a running account of their personal lives. They rose in popularity when services like LiveJournal and *Google's Blogger* started up in 1999. From 2007 to 2008, over 40 million blogs were created, giving us over 133 million blogs on the Web. (Technocrati, 2008)[37]

Blogs have become mainstream and are being used by nearly everyone, from political candidates such as Barack Obama to major CEOs such as Jonathan Schwartz (Sun Microsystems) and Craig Newmark (Craig's List). Even celebrities like David Beckham and Rosie O'Donnell find time to blog these days (or pay assistants to blog for them).

Types of Blogs

- **Personal.** A personal blog can be as simple as an online diary where you keep track of your life, or you can add commentary on your favorite topics and places of interest. You can also use your blog to detail your personal and professional achievements—wouldn't that be great to show prospective employers?

- **Business.** You may decide you want to start a blog that discusses what you do at your day job. Some corporate blogs are even endorsed on corporate websites. Entrepreneurs start business blogs to generate advertising revenue from banner ads or to attract new clients. Bloggers such as Darren Rowse (*www. problogger.net*) and Yaro Starak (*www.entrepreneurs-journey.com*) have found success through blogging, while other entrepreneurs use it as a revenue stream. If you're starting your own business venture, why not blog about it to the world?

- **Team.** If you have a group of friends or colleagues who share similar interests, then you have the ability to designate each an author who can post one or more times a week. The largest blogs typically have more than three bloggers. It's also a good way to expand your network and meet others with similar interests.

- **Schools.** Teachers are starting blogs to interact with students in a classroom setting. As part of assignments, students have to blog what they've learned the previous day or conduct research on a topic and blog about it. Interactive learning can happen anywhere and anytime through virtual classrooms.

- **Nonprofits.** Blogs such as the First Book Blog (*http://blog.firstbook.org*) offer daily commentary on what is going on in the organization, while providing a way for others to donate.

- **News.** One out of every four traditional journalists blog regularly, and individuals can be their own "citizen journalists," which means that you can play an active role in collecting and reporting news on your own blog (BRODEUR, 2008)[38]. Some major news outlets' websites now allow readers to share commentary on major news stories and events.

- **Aggregation.** Instead of writing posts, some individuals just copy and paste news off of other blogs or traditional news sites. The more technical bloggers build code to syndicate content on their blog with almost no effort. Maybe you can arrange a cross-promotional deal and agree to spread the word about other blogs in exchange for their promoting yours.

When it comes to your career and personal brand, a blog can either attract an audience directly or can become an addition to your resume. Through blogging, a job seeker can project a personal brand with a bio page, varied content, and much more. Whether you are an expert or "wannabe expert," a blog is a great starting point to promote your brand, expand your network, grow a community, and start conversations that may trigger opportunities. To be successful, you don't have to blog, but it can certainly help!

Blog Successfully

Here are some tips for successful blogging:

- Be passionate about a topic.
- Frequently post fresh content.
- Read and comment on other blogs.
- Network with other bloggers who share your passion.
- Be honest and open with your readership.

Don't write encyclopedia-style articles, because people can already find that information elsewhere—it's not distinctively *you*. Blogs are about clearly showing your voice and opinion on various topics. Once you establish trust with your readership, you will have a community of ambassadors that can help you find a job.

Google

Google is a personal brand search engine dynamo. People are constantly Googling topics to learn more about them, to find websites and images, get directions, and much more. One 20-year-old student Googled himself only to discover that the number one result was a news story that listed him as one of several people arrested on drug-related charges (*Globe* and *Mail*, 2008)[39]. Take a quick break from reading right now and Google yourself. Hopefully only positive things pop up!

> For those that embrace these new personal branding tools, 'Google me' is the new business card, and thus, the blog and social network profile is the new resume. Unlike the interview process, where the resume or self-description can be 'puffed,' the writings of a long-term blog demonstrates more about the individual.

—Jeremiah Owyang, senior analyst, Forrester Research

If you're not convinced of the power of Google, Careerbuilder. com reports that one out of five hiring managers conduct background checks on candidates using social networks, and 34% have dismissed a candidate based on what they've found[40]. You can bet that they're finding information from Google search results. One recruiter Googled a promising candidate and received a dating advertisement that the applicant had posted containing the line "Sex-related information could be seen as bizarre." Not surprisingly, it was decided the candidate wasn't a good fit for that corporate culture!

Before, after, or in between interviews, chances are you'll be Googled. Google results can either work for you or against you, and at some level, they cannot be controlled. It takes seconds to Google someone, and if your results are negative, you won't get the job. You may even want to Google the hiring manager to research his background before you arrive at an interview. It's a great way to develop an informed list of questions.

Virtual Worlds

A virtual world is a computer-based simulation of reality where users create and interact through *avatars*, which are 3D representations of their personal brands. *Second Life*, the most notable virtual world, boasts more than 12 million inhabitants since it launched in 2003.

Second Life has revolutionized the Internet and changed the landscape of recruitment, connecting passive and technical candidates with recruiters. Recruiters purchase land within the virtual world, construct a building, and create avatars for their corporate recruiting department to use to interview candidates. For example, American Apparel hired virtual sales clerks in Second Life, and TMP Worldwide Advertising & Communications held two virtual job fairs, which included employers from HP and Verizon (*BusinessWeek*, 2006)[43].

Aside from Second Life, there are other virtual worlds like MTV, where celebrities such as Lauren Conrad from *The Hills* make guest appearances, an Internet browser-based world (Second Life is an application). Recruiters can start conversations with qualified candidates whom they could never have reached before with this new medium. Simone Brunozzi was hired by Amazon.com after attending a virtual job fair to be a technology evangelist[44]. A virtual interview typically takes the place of a phone or first-round interview, and depending on the results, an in-person interview is set up with the applicant.

Entrepreneurs can be very successful in virtual worlds as well. One Second Life user, who generated assets worth more than $1 million in the real world, spent under $10 to get started. She achieved her fortune by purchasing small-scale virtual real estate, subdividing it, and developing the landscape for rental and resale (*IT World*, 2006)[45]. If you're not participating now, recognize that 80 percent of active Internet users will be in virtual worlds like Second Life by the end of 2011 (Gartner, 2007)[46].

Control Your Virtual World

Here are some basic virtual world tips:

- Before you register for Second Life, decide if you'll have enough time outside of work or school to participate, because just like video games, it's quite time consuming.

- When selecting an avatar, try your hardest to make it resemble your actual appearance.

- Handle virtual life just like real life, because every interaction can either help build or damage your personal brand.

Video Resumes

Video resumes are growing in popularity. They are often short video clips (less than three minutes) of candidates giving a summary of their credentials and positive attributes, and they should be treated like a real-life interview. According to a March 2007 survey conducted by Vault, 89 percent of employers would watch a video of a candidate to assess a candidate's professional presentation and demeanor. In addition, there are over 1,350 video resumes on YouTube as you're reading this, and that number will likely grow rapidly.

Typically, video resumes are filmed, edited, and uploaded to YouTube and/or embedded on your website or blog. Aside from promoting your video resume on YouTube and your own sites, you can include the URL within your resume or cover letter. If you're applying for a job in the entertainment industry or for a sales or marketing position, then video resumes will definitely differentiate you from others. Just make sure it represents you in a positive way or don't bother. Remember, everything you put out for public display represents your personal brand.

Create Your Video Resume

Here are some basic video resume tips:

- Practice many times before promoting your video resume. Remember that no one is forcing you to post it, so you have all the time in the world.

- Present yourself in proper business attire.

- Speak naturally as you are being recorded.

- Mention your name first, then your current position, your unique qualifications, and why someone should hire you for the job. Briefly summarize your experience as well.

- Be energetic and project confidence at all times, because no one wants to watch a video of a robot reciting sound bites.

Employer Branding

Employer branding is a term used for providing an online experience for potential candidates, employees, and other stakeholders with the goal of positively reinforcing the corporate image. According to Deloitte's "Competing for Talent" survey, the most critical talent issues facing organizations are attraction, development, and retention[48]. Successful HR organizations combat these issues by taking advantage of social media to attract and retain talent.

> **A company's brand is one of its strongest recruiting tools. Today people make their employment decisions based on a company's reputation and culture, as much as on salary, benefits, responsibilities, and other, more traditional criteria. Since attracting and retaining top talent is a crucial priority to companies in the global war for talent, a company's brand and its bottom line are irrevocably tied.**
>
> —Arie Ball, vice president of sourcing
> and talent acquisition, Sodexo

Companies that are using social media to their competitive advantage include Sodexho and Microsoft among a growing list of others. At present, they are still in the minority—only 26 percent of companies are currently implementing innovative recruitment strategies—but this figure should elevate dramatically over the next several years as big corporate machines come to realize the value in doing so.

- **Sodexo.** This leading provider of food and facilities management services has taken a major leap into using online networking for recruitment. It has its own YouTube podcast channel showing interns talking about available summer internships, which has been watched by over 5,000 people, as well as a blog and a presence in Second Life. Sodexho had 100 candidates express interest in the company after a meeting in Second Life of which 14 promising candidates received follow-up interviews after the event (ERE, 2007)[49].

- **Microsoft.** Microsoft has taken employer branding to a new level with *viewmyworld.com*, which is a collection of employee experiences and informative videos (including employment perks, office tours, and a cowboy named Roy who plays music while singing about new job opportunities). The intent of this new website is to give the giant corporation a more personal touch. Microsoft's Facebook page has over 44,000 fans, and the company has over 1,500 employee blogs on topics from Windows to Xbox.

Other companies can learn a lot from these forward thinkers. If they want to stay relevant in today's Web 2.0 world, they have to change their underlying processes. As Gen Y continues to pour into the workforce, companies will be forced to try new things to attract key talent, or they risk being upstaged by the competition.

As a brand, you need to have a presence where the corporate brands are playing and vice versa. That means you should create profiles where they are searching and recruiting, as well as exploring their high-tech venues. If you're entering the job market with a strong brand, you'll likely benefit from the emergence of social media. Starting a business from scratch is less challenging now because there are so many websites full of people waiting for opportunities. The hard part is finding the perfect match. You need to take full advantage of technological tools to achieve your optimal career goals.

Career Development

The rise of the Internet and the evolution of corporate expectations for employees have altered the way individuals develop within their careers. Now, instead of career development, there is personal brand management. College and career advisors may help you brainstorm career options or critique your resume, but their real value is in their networks and their connections to your school's alumni base. They have limited time to speak with each student, so always have a set agenda before meeting with them. The best possible outcome from a meeting with any advisor is a list of contacts so that you can set up informational interviews to learn more about the companies or positions that interest you.

Key Career Planning Questions

When planning your career path, ask yourself the following questions:

- What have I enjoyed learning about in college?

- What do I enjoy doing in my personal life?

- Where do I see myself in 3, 5, and 15 years?

- When do I want to start working? Should I go to graduate school?

- What skills do I have now, and which ones will I have to learn before I graduate?

- What type of corporate culture would suit my brand?

- Who in my network can assist me throughout my job search?

After speaking with various career advisors, the consensus is that applying for jobs on job boards is no longer enough. They are advising students to diversify their approach with networking—making a direct connection with their employers of choice. Advisors often refer to LinkedIn as a great tool for networking and locating job opportunities, and many warn students about putting improper pictures on Facebook. Career advisors realize that the Internet can serve as a gateway to life after college for many students.

“Most job or internship seekers will begin and end with opportunities that are posted on job boards or databases. I always tell students that they are selling themselves short if that's all that they do, considering that so many job and internship offers stem from leads through networking or contacts made directly with employers of interest.”

—Aileen Kyung Kim, assistant director of internships and career counseling, Princeton University

Many schools, such as American University, have taken the use of the Internet one step further by experimenting with Facebook and Second Life. American University has even hosted its very own social network, called the "inCircle Online Community," with the goal of attracting and retaining alumni for mentoring positions and possible job opportunities for recent graduates, as well as to build a protected community where students can build profiles and connect with others. Schools are starting to capitalize on the power of their own networks to e-launch student careers.

Relationship Networking

Traditional networking has advanced and expanded into social networking. Social networks are virtual sites built online, distributing content through collaboration and personal brands through messaging. In a global world, social networks allow you to reach across borders, share knowledge and experiences, and unearth new opportunities. Whether you demonstrate your mastery or genuine interest in a topic through photography, art, writing skill, personal information, video podcasts, or audio dialogues, social networking should be your medium.

We have all heard the phrase "It's not what you know, it's whom you know." With personal branding, this phrase changes to "It's not whom you know, it's who knows you." The more people who know you're alive, the better, even if you have never met them! If you walk into an interview and the hiring manager has already heard good things about you from a peer or read good things about you online, the likelihood you'll get hired is higher.

" To me, the opposite of networking is not working—every time you meet someone, you have an opportunity to learn from them or be a resource and give to them. It is all about giving first and building relationships. Networking is life. "

—Andrea Nierenberg, founder of The Nierenberg Group and author of *Million Dollar Networking*

Have you ever wondered why some people are able to seize job opportunities quickly, while others—perhaps yourself included—spend hours each day researching and applying to jobs with no outcome? Chalk it up to the power of networking.

Networking is an essential, effective communication skill—both in business and in one's personal life. A big part of the employee recruitment process is professionals connecting and forging potentially mutually beneficial relationships. It's been said that 80 percent of one's business comes from 20 percent of one's customers. Likewise, in your job search, you will ideally spend 80 percent of your time networking with the top 20 percent of those who can help you achieve your goals—your ideal network.

When job searching, successful networking can be a competitive advantage, because it can secure passage to a job even before it's posted for the nonconnected world to see. Internally, employees already know when a job is posted, who is hiring, whom to speak to, and how the process works. Of all available jobs, 80 percent are never advertised, and over half of all employees obtain their jobs through networking, according to BH Careers International (WSJ, 2005)[50]. Thus, a major objective in your career development should be to meet as many key people as you possibly can.

> ❝ I run a networking event for executives in my industry that is attended by over 150 people on a monthly basis and am always available by email to anyone and everyone who seeks my advice.... You never know where it can lead. ❞
>
> —Bill Sobel, principal, Sobel Media

I learned a valuable lesson about the importance of maintaining a strong network after graduating from college. I didn't have a sufficient network to achieve my immediate career goals quickly and spent a long time in "job search limbo." A few people I knew during college received job offers within weeks, often due to family members who held executive positions at companies, while I was submitting my resume to online job boards like Monster.com, at career fairs, through corporate submission websites, and to just about everyone I met. These attempts failed because I failed to realize that I was just one anonymous applicant among a crowd of others.

Think Beyond Online Job Listings

Applying to job listings online was a waste of my time. I was interviewing at jobs where the position was already taken, such as at Timberland, where they told me, "You've accomplished a lot at this young age," and then followed up, "but we've already filled the position." These experiences taught me a valuable lesson. I learned the importance of distinguishing myself from the crowd, of marketing myself so that I was the strongest candidate that I could possibly be, and to use networking so that the right people knew who I was.

If you leave networking out of your job search strategy, I guarantee that you will spend too much time applying for jobs that have already been taken. Why take the "impossible approach" when, through effective networking, you can land your dream job?

Here are your key networking channels:

- **School.** Meet people in classes in or associated with your major, work on projects with them, and get to know them the best you can. Use your school's career center and alumni network to your best advantage.

- **Organizations.** Join school organizations or outside special interest groups, attend regular meetings, and take a leadership position if you can.

- **Work.** Expand your horizons by finding people outside of your current work group and learn more about what their jobs entail. The more people you know in your specific career field, the better.

- **Online.** Conduct searches through social networks with criteria that match your interests. Join groups and register for events on Facebook and other major sites to expand your horizons.

- **Social.** Look at your social life as an unlimited opportunity to network. Every new interaction can open another door.

The *Network Strength Pyramid* (Figure 4.4) shows the relative positions and values of various connections that you can make as you go about making your career goals a reality. The stronger the relationship is between you and another person, the higher up that person will be in your pyramid.

Figure 4.4. The Network Strength Pyramid

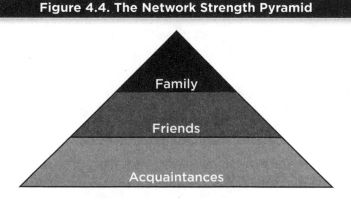

Family

Friends

Acquaintances

As you go from the bottom to the top of the pyramid, the chance of the individual going out of her way to help you get a job increases. This model suggests that family is the strongest connection. Nepotism aside, if your father is a director of marketing at Proctor & Gamble and an entry-level job opened up in the marketing research department, you will have a very good shot at first pass at that opportunity.

Friends are the next strongest layer in this pyramid, because good friends are more than willing to help you accomplish your goals. In certain companies, they might even be compensated, with a referral bonus, for helping you get the job!

Acquaintances are the weakest form of networking. Individuals who are hiring usually prefer to hire someone with whom they have closer ties over someone they just met. You have made many acquaintances throughout your life. Many will forget you over time, but you never know if one might come back into your life one of these days. You should strive to build relationships with your acquaintances and convert them into friends, but family members will often be your most valuable assets and can never be replaced. The networking guide in Figure 4.5 will show you how to network with each layer and what to watch out for.

Figure 4.5. Networking Guide

Layer	How to Network	What to Watch Out For
Family	• First, tell them what type of job you're looking for and then find out whom they know in those positions or companies. • You usually don't have to convince your family to help you out!	• If you are hired by a family member, your colleagues might be jealous or resentful. • Be sure to keep proving yourself and don't mention how you got the job, unless someone asks.

Figure 4.5. Networking Guide, continued.		
Layer	**How to Network**	**What to Watch Out For**
Friends	• Meet with your friends and find out what they do, how they like it, and if they can recommend you for a position. • Use your best judgment as to when and how you contact them. This is also a good test to see how tight your friendship is!	• Your friends might not have enough pull in their companies, especially if they just graduated college. • Just like your family, your success or failure is directly tied to their credibility and ability to select the right people.
Acquaintances	• When first meeting someone you don't know, find out as much as you can about him, before talking about yourself. • See if you can help them first; try to strengthen the relationship so they may become your friend.	• Don't be surprised if you never hear from them or if they aren't aggressively fighting for you to get a job. • It can be difficult to trust new acquaintances and for them to trust you, so set reasonable expectations.

Social Media

Social media has revolutionized networking. Social networking is deeply entrenched in personal branding, and as the Internet evolves, it is becoming an increasingly powerful tool to achieve your goals. Web 1.0 was private, secluded, and rigid; Web 2.0 is open, approachable, and welcoming. There are no more limitations on whom you can bond with and influence. As you browse the Internet, you will start to find websites that post email addresses, instant messenger (IM) names, and phone numbers freely.

I introduced you to social media in chapter 1; now it's time to go through the various social media applications. The terms *social media* and *social networking* are always being confused and used interchangably. A *social network* is one instance or example of social media: it is an online community of people who share similar interests. *Social media* is the great equalizer, giving everyone the same technology and capabilities.

> ❝ My blog, Customer Experience Matters, enables me to interact with so many people whom I never knew—and might never have known. The Internet provides both an open platform for self-expression and a highly searchable network. Together, they create a powerful foundation for social interactivity. ❞
>
> —Bruce Tempkin, Vice President and principal analyst, Forrester Research

In Web 1.0, you had to fill out an irritating contact form and never really knew whether it would reach the receiver's in-box or not. You now have the privilege of connecting with new people—with little effort. People who were once separated by layers of management are now "naked" on blogs and social networks, ready to respond to email. From CEOs to celebrities, people are not only easily found, but they want to be contacted and involved in the conversation. This means you can communicate with industry leaders, find mentors easily, and get jobs without applying for them.

Following are some examples of social media applications:

- **Collaboration.** Wikis are the ultimate collaborative tool. Many of you are familiar with Wikipedia, a moderated encyclopedia that is revised daily and whose entries include citations referencing news articles and research. Corporations such as Nokia estimate that at least 20 percent of their 68,000 employees use wiki pages to update schedules and project statuses and edit files (*BusinessWeek*, 2007)[51]. You can start your own wiki right now by going to *pbwiki.com* or *wikidot.com*. You can use the wiki as your to-do list for your life or to work on a document, such as a press release, with a colleague.

- **Communication.** Why use standard emails or phone calls when you can talk through social networks or *Twitter*? Millennials are the captains of this new form of communication. Facebook, the current leading social network, allows you to instant message your friends, send messages as you would emails, and even post on your friends' "walls." Twitter, noted as a microblogging service, allows you to create an account and follow your friends' accounts to receive their updates. You can then message all your friends at once. The more people who follow your account, the more people will receive each message you send.

  Both Twitter and Facebook allow you to communicate real-time through your mobile phone. Corporations are using social networks internally to be more productive, reduce email, and please Gen Y employees and customers. For example, KPMG has a 10,000-person social network for its former employees, who often refer business to their former company, and Starbucks captures customer's ideas with its My Starbucks Idea social network (*BusinessWeek*, 2007)[52].

- **Multimedia.** When blogging or twittering isn't enough, there is always photo and video. *Flickr* allows you to upload, tag, organize, and share your digital photos, and YouTube is the equivalent for videos. As of January 2008, YouTube had 77.6 million viewers, which is one-third of all online viewers in the United States. YouTube visitors watched more than three billion user-posted videos, according to comScore Inc[53].

Social media invites everyone in the world to be part of the online discussion, including *you*. Our voices can finally be heard, and we can have a lot of fun sharing multimedia or messaging through a social network. The tools are out there for you to use, and they are all free.

Search Engine Optimization (SEO)

Search engines are how people find information. In 2008, almost half of Internet users used search engines on a typical day, up from one-third in 2002 (Pew Internet & American Life Project)[54]. *Search engine optimization* (SEO) is the process of using search engines to increase the traffic at a specific website.

Google founders Larry Page and Sergey Brin developed *PageRank™*, which is the core component of their engine. Page-Rank relies on links as indicators of site authority and popularity. The PageRank scale is 0–10, and sites that have a 5 or above generally have thousands of back-links (sites linking to them). If you already have a website, then go to *pr.blogflux.com* to check your own PageRank.

Also, the sites linking back to your site have to have content that is somewhat relevant to your website and have a high importance of their own. When Google indexes your page, it crawls all the links in and out of your webpage. Aside from links, Google pinpoints the number of times a search term appears on a given website to see if it's a good match for a query.

Two areas on each search page contain links to websites—natural and paid:

> **1: Natural.** In the main content section, which sits on the left-hand side of a search page, you will see ten results. Each one of these websites has earned its spot and is respected by the searcher. *Natural search*, sometimes called "organic," is far more popular than paid and doesn't cost you money. An average of 9.2 search results are viewed before the first click, and since people spend 10.4 seconds on a page to view search results, your goal is be in the top three results (Checkit and De Vos & Janse 2007)[55].

> **2: Paid.** This form of pay-per-click (PPC) advertising shows up on the right-hand side of your search page. With *paid search,*webmasters pay a price each time a user clicks on

their links. Some key words are more valuable than others because people search for them more, which means they cost the site owner more money per click. If you aren't at the top of the search results, a paid advertising link may be a solution.

You need to build your personal branding strategy around search engines because that's how people find information and other people. In chapter 8, I will show you how to control your results and reputation in search engines using the top SEO strategies.

Entrepreneurship

It doesn't matter if you're 16 or 60, you can be a successful entrepreneur. To be an entrepreneur, be someone who takes risks, is confident, and seeks to succeed at the highest level. A successful entrepreneur is someone who sees a need in the marketplace, starts her own business, and holds some degree of accountability and liability for the inherent risks.

Successful Young Entrepreneurs

- **Ben Cathers** was 12 when he started a Web marketing and advertising firm targeting teenagers, which grew into two offices with ten employees.

- **Daniel Brusilovsky** was 15 when he started a "Teens in Tech" community for teenagers interested in producing and sharing social media content in a safe environment.

- **Kristopher Tate** was 17 when he founded an online photo-sharing site.

- **Nancy Montano** was 22 when she launched Los Angeles Pumping, a hazardous waste company.

- **Ryan Allis** was 21 when he grew his email marketing company, iContact, to 1 million in sales.

- **Rob Kalin** was 28 when he launched Etsy, which is now the largest online marketplace for people to buy and sell handmade crafts.

Not everyone is born to be an entrepreneur. Over the past few decades, the media has brainwashed us into thinking that most start-up companies fail. Guess what? According to the U.S. Office of Advocacy, approximately two out of every three start-ups survive at least two years (Small Business Association, 2005)[56]. Almost half survive at least four years. If you have a business idea in high school, college, or at any time in your life, follow your dreams and try to make it happen! If you wish to be an entrepreneur as a young adult, realize that one of your greatest challenges will be to get taken seriously by people older than you. You can make this happen: always have confidence and a positive attitude, believe in yourself and your ideas, and work hard.

Five Tips for Succeeding as a Young Entrepreneur

1: **Have a plan—and a backup plan.** Let's face it; there is a chance that your business could fail, but knowing that, you can protect yourself. Some entrepreneurs juggle a full-time job and a business on the side, in hopes the business idea will take off and become the full-time job. Even if the business fails, you will gain many new experiences, extend your skills, and learn from mistakes, which can shorten the learning curve for your next business. Diversification, like investing in different stocks, is important to your success. Although some stocks might plummet, others may grow to balance off your returns. So if your first idea doesn't work out, try another one!

2: **Surround yourself with greatness.** If you are looking for a partner to help you start your business or to hire employees, try to recruit people who are capable and intelligent and offer something that complements your skill set. Your business will be stronger as a result.

3: **Be up for the challenge.** If running a business were easy, everyone would do it. But as you may have noticed, most people are working for other companies. When you own your own business, you have to deal with customers and clients contacting you at every hour of the day and always be analyzing market trends and competitors to stay ahead of the curve—among a ton of other things. If you're going to do this, make sure you're ready for all the work that you need to put into a business to make it successful.

4: **Gather available resources.** Many young entrepreneurs don't have a lot of capital, but there are many other resources out there for you. Use your existing network to help you (maybe you have a friend who can develop your websites or family members who can help fund your business?) and use your networking skills to meet others who are in a position to help.

5: **Keep organized.** You never want to miss a deadline, especially if your excuse was that you flew to Cancun with your college buddies. Try to separate your professional and personal lives and keep track of all the things you need to get done each day (prioritizing your to-do list is a great idea) while overseeing the daily operations of your business. Purchase a calendar or personal digital assistant, or use Microsoft Outlook or another online calendar tool, to mark down appointments, goals, and pending tasks.

The world of work and the way we have to manage our careers is breaking away from the past. As millennials, we have a great opportunity to make a difference and show companies what we're made of.

Now that you've learned about the history and topics that concern personal branding, you are ready for commander training! This consists of a proven four-step process that will help you discover, create, communicate, and maintain your personal brand for a successful career:

1: **Discover.** In the discover step, you will learn about yourself, figure out what makes you distinctive, and learn how to develop the right skills.

2: Create. In the create step, you will build a complete marketing kit that you can use in interviews or when networking.

3: Communicate. In the communicate step, you will take everything you've created and learn how to promote it to others.

4: Maintain. In the maintain step, you will perform routine maintenance so that your reputation is monitored and protected.

The more we learn and concentrate on living up to our potential, the more we can add our unique value to our careers.

Part II: Command Your Career in Four Steps

Chapter 5

Step 1—Discover Your Brand

After graduating from college in 2006, I devoted almost 100 percent of my attention toward refining and leveraging my personal brand for career success. During this time, my personal brand was shaped by all my encounters in the corporate world, including meetings, on-the-job training, and instructor-led classes. My goal was to climb the corporate ladder and see how much I could accomplish in the least amount of time possible. Use the lessons I've learned to help you discover brand YOU and achieve your career goals

Take Chances—and Learn from the Results

In 2006, I launched my first blog. At the time, Google was a predominant force in blogging with its Blogger platform, and I used this free service to launch my blog, entitled "Driven-To-Succeed." My blog detailed my experiences confronting the recruitment cycle and the valuable lessons I learned as a result. My insights were catalogued in a series of posts such as "Dress for Success" and "Getting Your First Job" and included a few helpful visuals. My original intent was to convey what I'd learned to others who wanted to achieve their career goals.

The bottom line was that no one knew who I was. Regardless of how good my advice was, it wasn't going to be effective unless it hit people's radar. I had not promoted the blog, nor had I developed a community. I was building my brand without an audience. As a result, aside from the occasional comment, I received very little response or feedback. Before long, I stopped posting. Driven-To-Succeed quickly disintegrated into thin air.

Your Brand Needs an Audience!

Regardless of how incredible your brand is, if you fail to promote it and link it to the right audience, it has little chance of succeeding.

This unfortunate event might have deterred others from trying again, but I was determined to learn from my missteps and turn my failures into successes. I studied various other blogs around my topic to learn what worked and what didn't. This really helped me develop skills that translated into my future success with personal branding, and I highly recommend you take this approach when developing your brand.

During this time, I experienced both personal and professional doubt—and social pressure. I spent years trying to figure out who I was, how I should dress, how to interact with others, and what my lifelong objectives were. I was afraid to settle on one career path and isolate myself from other opportunities. I also felt uncertainty toward the current job market. My network was thin, and I wasn't in a position to make any drastic moves, especially with meager finances. I was probably a lot like you.

The key is not to let these issues turn into obstacles. Look at them as action items—things to add to your to-do list and conquer.

- **Unsure about how to dress to brand yourself for success?** Look at how others dress in your chosen field for some tips.

- **Unsure about how to network?** Watch how the pros do it and give it a shot. You'll get better as you gain experience and learn what works for you.

- **Confused about your future goals?** Take some time to discover who you really are and to link your skill set and passions with the path that's right for you.

Each issue you settle will bring you closer to discovering your perfect personal brand!

It won't happen overnight. I exhausted many years trying to discover myself. Then, in 2007, that day came when I was introduced to personal branding. I was surfing the Internet, searching for marketing websites to research current trends. Tom Peters's article first appeared during my search for personal branding information, along with a few blogs that had posts on the subject. While reading the article, I realized that Tom's points resembled some of my own marketing philosophies:

- **Everyone** needs to be the CEO of his own brand, because at the end of the day, we must have control over our own careers to achieve success.

- **Everyone** can turn a successful project into bargaining power with management to secure a higher salary.

- **Everyone** will experience setbacks on her path to building brand YOU, but after you discover yourself and start taking control, a snowball effect will trigger more and more opportunities.

- **Everyone** has a chance to stand out, learn, improve, and build his skills.

At this moment, I discovered that my passion was, in fact, personal branding. As I developed my personal branding strategy and started sharing it, personal branding became less about me and more about others. Before, I would wake up every morning and say to myself, "I want to make the largest impact in the least amount of time." Now I say, "I want to help others avoid the mistakes I made and find real success and happiness in their lives."

It's time to teach you how to discover your own brand. First we'll assess your current situation. Then you'll learn about the three personal branding elements and fill out a development plan as well as a *personal marketing plan*.

Invest in Personal Discovery

The goal of this phase is discovery—to learn more about yourself, where you are right now, and where you want to be in the future. This is an essential step toward determining your brand and developing a plan to move forward.

> " My relationship with myself affects how I see every person I know. Before I can build a foundation of concrete where I can stand and leave room for others to be who they are, I have to know my core strengths and values, especially that one big idea—that value that wraps within it all other bits I believe in. Soon the folks who do business with me know that I'm the one they can count on to keep that promise. Branding is knowing who I am. "
>
> —Liz Strauss, founder of SOBCon and Successful Blog

You can start by asking yourself, "Who am I?" This question seems simple enough, but the truth is that most people don't truly find out who they are until later in life. Along the way, many people switch colleges, majors, and careers multiple times. Why is there so much change and uncertainty? Because discovering yourself—who you truly are and what you want out of life—can be a difficult process. The discovery phase of my personal branding strategy is designed to help you do this. Once you discover yourself, developing your brand will be that much easier.

Personal Discovery Assessment

Ask yourself the following questions to help figure out who you are and what career path might be right for you.

- What are my five favorite activities?
- What are the top five personality attributes I'd use to describe myself?
- What are the top five personality attributes that others use to describe me?
- What personal attributes would you like to improve?
- What classes were your favorites in college?
- What classes were your least favorite in college?
- What are the key elements of a successful career, in your opinion?

Taking the time to invest in personal brand discovery will allow you to focus and prepare for what lies ahead. When I was growing up, I waited a long time to figure out exactly who I was and what I wanted to do, and I paid the price—wasted time and effort. Do yourself a favor; learn from my mistakes and work hard to avoid them!

Now that you know a little more about yourself, take some time to think about what you'd like your brand to tell the world. As previously stated, a great place to start is to look at all the brands you've encountered in your life. Take the following quiz with this in mind.

> ## Brand Discovery Assessment
>
> Ask yourself the following questions to help figure out ways to develop your effective personal brand:
>
> - What would you like to accomplish with your brand?
>
> - Who is your target audience?
>
> - What brand elements do you think your target audience would respond favorably to?
>
> - What brand elements do you think your target audience would respond poorly to?
>
> - Which brands do you think are successful? Why are they successful?
>
> - What brand elements would best showcase your specific talents and skill set?

Keep in mind that your brand is a constant work in progress, one that changes and evolves as you grow and learn more about yourself.

Controlling Your Personal Brand Perception

Your personal brand is a reflection of two perspectives—your own perception of yourself and others' impressions of you. People will label you throughout your life. They may use phrases such as *hard worker*, *slacker*, or *gifted*. The way others describe you is based on the experience they've had with you. Pay attention to these descriptors and assess how they align with your own perception. Then work toward ensuring that both your perception and the world's perception of you—and your personal brand—are positive ones.

Take a close look at the list of negative workplace descriptors in Figure 5.1. Have you or your coworkers used any of these to describe you? If so, then think of ways to correct the negative and turn it into a positive.

Figure 5.1. Workplace Descriptors		
Negative	**How to Correct the Negative**	**Positive**
Lazy	• Communicate with your manager regularly, clearly citing all the work you have finished. • Take the initiative; go above and beyond your current assignments to emphasize your productivity.	Productive
Obnoxious	• Show respect by being courteous to others, not interrupting in meetings, and not bothering your coworkers when they are busy.	Courteous
Messy	• Make sure your work area is clean at all times, using file folders to sort papers and putting them in drawers if possible. • Avoid being the person who's always forgetful, late to meetings, and ill prepared.	Organized
Distracted	• Avoid work distractions whenever possible and close all nonwork-related websites at work unless you are on a lunch break. • IM only if your coworkers are doing so to communicate.	Focused
Reliant	Ask for work that is outside of your usual tasks and comfort zone. Take charge of projects to learn how to be self-sufficient.	Self-sufficient

Gain Confidence in Yourself

Many people out there are incapable of finding a job and a pathway to successful living. If this is you, then you might be lacking one of the most important factors in brand discovery—confidence. Confidence will make or break your self-esteem, your ability to communicate, and your opportunities for success in life.

> **"** Confidence comes from making mistakes. The more mistakes you make, the more you know what not to do. **"**

—Steve Tatham, staff writer, Walt Disney

Confidence is key in a variety of life situations, including these:

- Professional networking
- Giving a presentation at work
- Meeting new people in social situations
- Impressing your boss
- Working on a group project at work or in school

A positive side effect of brand discovery is that by learning more about who you are and what you'd like to accomplish, you discover what you need to improve in your life. If you think that a lack of confidence may be holding you back, consider the following confidence-boosting strategies:

- **Remind yourself of past successes.** Confidence grows with every success you have. For instance, if you get straight As during your sophomore year of college, you will have the confidence needed to get them again junior year. In contrast, a student used to failing might have given up hope. Recall the times in your life when you experienced success and the good feelings you had, then transfer those feelings into your current mind-set.

- **Confront your insecurities.** You need to confront your insecurities head on and tackle them. This could be anything from acne to regrets. Start by identifying them, writing them down, and telling yourself that you won't let them keep you from achieving your goals.

- **Remember that no one is perfect.** Everyone feels as though they are lacking something at some point. Keep telling yourself that these feelings are normal and they're nothing to get depressed over. Life is full of hardships and challenges, but they help build our characters.

- **Be thankful for what you have.** Sometimes you might feel as though you don't have enough of something, such as money or friendships. But the truth is that a lot of people have less than you do. Learn to appreciate what you have.

- **Concentrate on strengths, not weaknesses.** Since confidence comes from within, you need to have positive energy. This comes with doing what you love and what you are good at. Try writing down at least ten positive things about yourself.

- **Embrace yourself and your true potential.** Everyone in the world is special, including you! Love yourself for who you are, always keep in mind that things will get better if you work on them, and never, ever, lose hope.

- **Find a confident role model.** Find someone who has the confidence level you'd like to have and model some of his behaviors. Try speaking with him or her and getting advice, because he or she must be doing something right.

Be Persistent

Persistence is an inherent desire to achieve a specific goal, no matter what it takes. If you're confident about your brand, you're more willing to go the extra mile to sell it.

Most success stories you hear about are about those who have endured obstacles along the way, learned from their mistakes, and achieved excellence. They persisted in the face of discouragement and learned from the mistakes they've made. Richard Branson is a great example; he failed exams at school, had business ventures fail, failed in attempts to go around the world in a hot air balloon, and even went into serious debt during his life. Today, he is worth billions, and his Virgin brand name includes a fleet of over 360 companies.

Want to add a little persistence to your life? Follow these simple steps:

1: **Set a goal.** Before you invest your energy in something, realize what your desired outcome is. Knowing this will help you create the best plan of attack.

2: **Timing is key.** Decide the best time to pursue success. Learn a lesson from our "friends" who call us on the phone to sell us things. When they interrupt you during dinner, how likely are you to purchase the product?

3: **Be prepared.** In business, time is money, and people are almost always busy. Half the battle is just showing up prepared! If you want to accomplish your goals, have a firm agenda of what you want to get done and a strategy for making it happen.

4: **Follow up.** If at first you don't succeed, try, try again.

5: **Create a win-win.** Everyone loves to win, so if you can figure out how your target audience can benefit, you will be more successful at getting their attention and achieving your goals.

6: **Take a hint.** If all else fails, leave the person alone. You can't force people to do anything, and after a few attempts, you'll get a clear signal that she won't respond or isn't interested. Move on when the time is right.

Personal branding is for those who want to create a powerful presence and a memorable identity to have a positive effect on the world. A powerful brand is one that leaves others with a positive perception.

The Three Key Elements of Effective Personal Branding

There are three key elements of effective personal branding:

1: A strong *personal value statement*

2: **A plan to differentiate your brand** from that of the competition

3: **A powerful** *marketing strategy*

In the following sections, I examine each element and provide examples and an action plan for you to incorporate into your brand.

Create a Strong Personal Value Statement

In a nutshell, your personal value statement is what you stand for. The brands you purchase, consume, work for, and endorse are all part of your promise of value. They are each unique components that make up who you are as a brand. For example, if you attend Harvard Business School, people will tend to view you as an intellectual and an attractive candidate for a job without even seeing your grades or the classes you've taken. The Harvard brand will be part of your signature for life, and the network that is tied to the brand will always open doors for you.

When you meet someone for the first time, your initial impression is undoubtedly affected by your opinion of each of the brands with which they are associated. If your opinions are positive, then your impression will be relatively favorable. If they're negative, then that person is at an unfortunate disadvantage. The message here is that the company you work for, as well as how you dress, drive, and behave, are key factors that make up how others perceive you. To put it another way, the total equity of the brands you choose to associate with and support is reflected in your personal brand.

Brand Impression

Each brand has various attributes, values, and perceptions tied to it. Think of a woman who:

- drives a **Mercedes**, one of the world's premier automotive brands.

- wears **Lacoste** clothing, a high-end French apparel brand recognized by its green crocodile logo.

- works for **General Electric**, a global technology and service conglomerate and one of the world's most powerful corporate brands.

What is your initial impression of this woman based on your impressions of these brands?

Research has shown that it takes less than 30 seconds for someone to form a lasting impression of you. If you make a poor first impression, it can take up to 21 interactions to institute a better one. Make your first impression count!

When you interview for a certain position, think about what your experience and background is conveying. If you have previously worked for a well-known brand, such as GE, you will likely be taken more seriously. The interviewer will associate your name with that of the larger company and may attribute the company's success to you. The more "strong brands" you have on your resume, the stronger your brand will be. Let this association work in your favor. Remember, all the brands that surround you play a role in building your own brand.

Following are the benefits of being associated with major brands:

- **Awareness.** People have heard, seen, and touched them, so you won't have to work hard to convey an impression of the brand.

- **Credibility.** Having the name on your resume will indicate that you were worthy of employment there, passing all requirements and assessments. Let's face it; it's often tough to get a job at a large company because of the stiff competition a strong brand name attracts. If you land the job, you get to use the name as an endorsement for brand *You*.

- **Status.** From my experience, you can leverage your big-brand experience much more easily than experience with an unknown brand. For example, it's easier for people who work for big brands to get speaking opportunities at conferences and get quoted in the media.

Don't have a big brand name behind you? Here's what you can do:

- **Pitch yourself as a jack-of-all-trades.** Small businesses give you more flexibility and diverse work opportunities that can really round out your experience and skill set.

- **Have a good understanding of the companies for which you have worked.** The person to whom you are talking might not have heard of these companies before. You have an opportunity to show how much you know.

- **Lead with actual work experiences you've had.** Instead of focusing on the brands on your resume, try to pull together school projects or organizations where you were a leader. This experience can really help you to stand out.

In today's business world, your value statement also includes the people who surround you. Whom you deal with on a recurring basis has an effect on your brand. Their brand perception brushes off onto yours, either favorably or unfavorably. Depending on your specific goals, if you associate with CEOs or well-regarded businesspeople, people will likely have more respect for your brand than if you keep company with teenagers or unemployed individuals.

As you start discovering and developing your brand, make note of your appearance, personality, and skills—not just at work or important functions but at all times. You never know whom you're going to run into.

These key areas will help you identify who you are and control your brand perception.

Appearance

Your personal appearance is a combination of your dress, behavior, and body language. The first impression that your audience forms of your appearance is critical to your brand perception, acceptance, and credibility. For example, if you dress in a suit, stand with good posture, and act professionally, you will likely be viewed positively. A key factor in having brand *You* perceived positively is understanding your intended audience. Thus, you should be keenly aware of what style of appearance your target audience will best respond to. The chart in Figure 5.2 highlights ways in which people moderate their appearance to fit the situation.

Figure 5.2. Adapting Your Appearance		
Situation	**Appropriate Appearance**	**Inappropriate Appearance**
Wedding	Tuxedo Dress	If you show up in a bathing suit or a ripped shirt, you might get asked to leave immediately. A wedding is a serious event, and people set high expectations for clothing and behavior.
Rock Concert	Jeans Hat T-shirt	Anything too formal will be judged harshly. Plus, you may stain your clothing. Rock concerts are social venues and usually not a place for business.

Situation	Appropriate Appearance	Inappropriate Appearance
Business Presentation	Suit Tie Blouse Skirt	If you wear a dirty, wrinkled shirt or a too-short skirt, management will be distracted by your poor choices and not focus on your delivery.
Company Party	Button-down shirt Dress pants Blouse Skirt	When you go out with your fellow employees, you want to appear fun and gregarious—in moderation. If you show up too formally, then you may be implying that you don't know how to have fun.

Think of your appearance as product packaging: you want it to be the best reflection of your talents and abilities as possible. Various stereotypes are associated with appearance, some of which you can control and use to your advantage, and some you cannot avoid because they are buried in our culture. For instance, if you wear a tie-dyed shirt, forget to shave, and smell like beer from last night's house party, you just might have difficulty meeting new people. Keep this in mind as you develop your brand image.

> A person who comes to work dressed in an appropriate manner will surpass someone who comes to work looking disheveled. If a person does not take pride in his or her own appearance and image, many employers may believe they will not represent their company well.

—Lindsay Liles, producer, E! Networks

Figure 5.3 gives some recommended strategies for presenting a strong, positive brand image when faced with a specific situation—a first interview.

Figure 5.3. Attire for the First Interview	
Men	**Business suit.** For men, this is a set expectation for an interview, unless the hiring manager tells you otherwise. I've personally been asked to dress business casual in a few interviews where the company culture is more relaxed. Your suit should be well tailored and of precise size and length. You can't afford to be sloppy, and investing in a quality suit will enhance your confidence and help you make that great first impression. **Suit colors.** Acceptable colors are dark shades of grays, blues, and black. You can wear pattern designs as well, with pinstripes or plaids. Pay special attention to the season and climate, because you should wear lighter clothing in the summer and darker in the winter. **Shirt.** Wear a plain white or off-white shirt or pastel shades of blue, pink, or yellow. Look conservative and not too flashy. **Necktie.** A striped, dotted, or paisley tie in any color that complements your suit, shirt, or both will work just fine. **Shoes and socks.** Make sure your shoes are shined before your interview. Loafers are too casual, so wear laced shoes if you can. The color of your socks should complement the rest of your outfit. Don't wear argyle or see-through socks.
Women	**Business suit.** Just like males, females should dress conservatively to present a professional image. Your skirt length should not be too long or short. **Suit colors.** Women can get away with wearing brighter colors, including reds, blues, and greens. You can also wear different fabrics and still be professional. **Blouse.** It should complement your suit and be conservative. That means it shouldn't be too revealing, high around the neck, or have many ruffles. White is your best bet to complement your suit colors. **Stockings.** Wear flesh-toned stockings and avoid any distracting colors. **Shoes.** Don't try to make a "statement" by wearing overly high heels. Go for the professional look to match everything else.

Regardless if you are in an interview, a night out on the town, or at a hockey game, good posture and a positive attitude will complement anything you wear. Body language says a lot about you as well, so practice standing up straight, making good eye contact, and keeping your head up.

Personality

Your personality—including your ability to communicate and interact with your peers and colleagues—is a key component of your brand identity. It reflects the sort of person you are, and it indicates to others what it would be like to spend time with you, work alongside you, enter into a business deal with you, and have to rely upon you.

> Social media offers a way to make your personality an asset for your career. As more and more people recognize this, the necessity for personal branding will only continue to grow.

—Rohit Bhargava, Senior VP of marketing, Ogilvy Digital, and author of *Personality Not Included*

The following exercise should make it clear how important it is to ensure that others have a positive initial impression of you. Your personality is like a magnet, attracting others to your brand—or repelling them.

Personality can be developed over time, as you gain life experience and maturity. Ideally, your personality should suit the situation in which you envision yourself: if you are a comedian, you need a charismatic and humorous personality, whereas if you are a librarian, your personality should convey seriousness, thoroughness, and professionalism.

Personality Trait Exercise

In the following table, write down what you feel your initial impression would be as you started working with someone with each of the following personality traits:

Personality Trait	Initial Impression
Dense	
Egomaniacal	
Conscientious	
Demanding	
Dependable	
Detail-oriented	

Keep the following tips in mind:

- **Analyze your audience.** Make a quick decision about how you should act based upon the first few seconds of your interaction. You can tell a lot by someone's facial expression and introduction cues—even her handshake strength is a cue. Then react accordingly.

- **Stay self-aware.** When interacting, think about how you are being perceived. If you are too vocal, aggressive, and excited, it might work against you. Look for cues from your audience; you can tell when someone genuinely cares and wants to listen to you and when he is losing interest. Respond accordingly and keep your audience engaged.

Professional Skills

Among the most valuable skills to develop when forming your personal brand—to help you interview, network, and achieve your career goals—are written and verbal communication skills and technical skills. Each skill set supports the another and contributes to the overall strength of brand YOU.

One of the most important methods of communication is writing. Your writing may appear in emails, blogs, papers, reports, presentations, or websites. If your writing is unclear, with poor grammar and sentence structure, you risk losing credibility and respect, along with the opportunity to convey important information and spread your brand messaging. Strong writing skills are vital to a successful career—if you can't write in a clear-cut fashion, you will lose opportunities for success.

Think of all the emails and text messages you send in a single day. What if the recipients are unable to understand what you are trying to say? That's a lot of wasted time and effort on both sides, and in the professional world, that time and effort means lost money and opportunities.

In addition to writing well, you need to maintain different sets of writing skills for different occasions. For example, your ability to write superbrief, hyperabbreviated messages to your friends may be a valuable networking skill, whereas being able to develop a clear and detailed project plan might serve you well at your job or when trying to attract potential investors for your start-up business.

Here are some tips for better business writing:

- **Know your audience.** Are you writing to your boss, a colleague, or a friend? In general, the closer your relationship is with your audience, the more casual you can be with your writing. Assess your reader's technical background before using terms like *megabyte* and *router*. Be conscious of your tone and message goals before you send an email to someone you've never met before. Don't write an instant message to an executive when she is expecting a detailed email.

- **Use formatting.** Most people don't have time to read through long emails if they aren't broken down and clearly structured. Try adding headings, subheadings, and bulleted lists to organize your writing and help guide and engage your audience. If you're designing promotional and marketing materials for your business or writing copy for your website, keep in mind that your messaging should be as attractive and inviting as it is informative. How your messaging appears is crucial to your brand image.

- **Look before you leap.** The best way to begin is to think carefully about what messages and overall impression you want your writing to give your target audience.

- **Review and revise.** After writing your first draft, go back and reread it to make sure you highlighted all the points you wanted to get across. Check for grammar, spelling, and punctuation errors. Make sure each sentence flows smoothly into the next. And try reading it aloud to make sure it has the tone and clarity you want. It's great if you can have someone else review your work—a fresh set of eyes always helps. It may take several attempts to get it just right, but it's worth the effort, and the more you practice, the better you'll get.

Effective verbal communication is another important skill. Interpersonal communication is valuable in networking, accomplishing tasks, and getting others to have confidence in your brand. Communication skills are employed in speeches, presentations, day-to-day conversation with peers—even in elevator pitches to executives who are looking for the next new business idea—and each interaction is important to showcasing your personal brand in a positive light. Through effective communication, you can build credibility, network effectively, and earn the trust and respect of those whose opinions really matter.

Remember, your credibility is at stake during any verbal exchange. You will be graded based on what you say and how you say it. This is why preparation is the key to your success.

If possible, be aware of your audience's preferences before approaching them, whether in person, over the phone, or through email or text message. Be flexible from the beginning and adapt to your audience's likes and dislikes, even when choosing the method of communication; some prefer phone or email communication, while others like IM, Skype, or one of the many other social networking options available. Is your audience playful and appreciative of humor, or do they like to get right down to business? The key is to know your audience and try to communicate in the way that will work to your best advantage.

Here are some tips for enhancing your verbal communication skills:

- **Listening.** By listening effectively, you gather information about your audience. Look for physical as well as verbal cues and modulate your exchange accordingly.

- **Pace yourself.** Speak at a pace that matches your audience's preference and style. Always allow them to soak up everything they need to make a decision. If they seem to need more clarification, or if they seem impatient, react accordingly.

- **Ask questions.** No one knows everything. If you fail to comprehend part of the conversation, then ask as many questions as you can or risk embarrassment later. If your boss gives you an assignment, ask questions to uncover all the information you need to complete the project successfully. Asking questions also shows that you care about the other people involved in the discussion and what they have to say.

- **Enunciate and animate.** Don't talk in a monotone. Speaking dynamically, while still maintaining an aura of professionalism, can inspire confidence and keep your audience interested. Don't forget, you need to speak clearly and judge your volume based on the number of people you're talking to and the environment you're in. If you're sitting next to someone, turn down your volume, but if you are in a stadium with hundreds of people, speak louder.

- **Vocabulary matters.** People will judge your intelligence based on your vocabulary. Are you trying to convince your audience that you're knowledgeable in a certain area? Be sure to have a solid grasp of common industry lingo. You don't want to use words that are so unfamiliar that you don't put them in the proper context, or appear as though you're trying too hard. Start to learn a word a day to build your vocabulary.
- **Body language counts.** Your hand gestures and facial expressions will influence your audience, so be aware of what your body language is saying.

Technical skills are not only as important as written and verbal communication skills, they are mandatory for career competence in today's world. Most jobs require experience using software packages such as Microsoft Office for performing daily tasks, from preparing documents and presentations to scheduling meetings and sending email. Depending on your career goals, many jobs require more specific technical knowledge and expertise.

To improve the strength of your brand, you should invest time in improving your technical skills and keeping them current. Make note of the skills that are often required in your particular field and be sure you have them. If you are comfortable in one technical area, push yourself out of your comfort zone and breathe new life into your brand by learning something new. I did this by experimenting with social media outside of work and learning how to post and comment on my own. You should take the same approach.

Here are some tips for enhancing your technical skills:

- **Research.** Find out what technical skills are required for your job by searching the Web or asking people who are already in that field. Go to websites such as *w3schools.com* and *elementk.com* and browse through the skills that relate to your field. Make the most of available online tutorials or consider taking a course.

- **Books.** Go to *amazon.com* and purchase technical books, such as a book on HTML or Microsoft PowerPoint. I also recommend the *For Dummies* series. These guides are very informative and easy to follow.

- **Find tech experts.** Some people were born with a technical mind. If you aren't such a person or friends with one, it's time to start meeting people who can help you learn technical skills.

- **Create a website.** Everyone should know how to create a website, especially if starting a new business venture. If you have no experience, then turn to *sites.google.com*, where you can learn to build a website in the same way you'd write a paper in Microsoft Word (you'll need a Google account if you don't already have one, but signing up is free and only takes a moment).

Differentiate Your Brand

As a brand, you have strengths and weaknesses just like everyone else. These attributes allow you to stand out from those around you. They are your differentiators.

Your differentiators are one of the most important parts of your personal brand. If you were a recruiter, would you want to hire an unremarkable candidate? No. You would seek out an individual who possesses exceptional abilities that no other applicants demonstrated. When salespeople try to close a deal, they communicate a clear differentiator that will convince consumers that they are buying a superior product. You are the primary salesperson for your brand, so take the same approach.

Be a Purple Cow!

Seth Godin describes the "purple cow" theory in his book *Purple Cow: Transform Your Business by Being Remarkable* (Portfolio, 2003)[58]. Imagine driving down a highway, passing a farm, and spotting a purple cow. Wouldn't that be remarkable? To be a purple cow means to be indispensible, astonishing, and buzz worthy. You wouln't react the same way if the cow had traditional black and white coloring would you? Of course not.

Use your unique life experiences to differentiate your brand. Examples of such differentiators include winning an award, being named to a society, or working for a philanthropic organization. All of these examples contribute to your brand value.

Ask yourself the following questions:

- What makes me special?
- What do people in my network think is special about me?
- Have I ever been complimented for a particular skill or talent?
- Is there something I do well and am passionate about?
- What achievements in my life am I most proud of?

When I was looking for my first job in marketing, I found that my eight marketing internships were a valuable differentiator, especially since I had been able to manage them alongside the responsibilities of school and leadership positions in seven extracurricular organizations. You should always work toward expanding your horizons—it will really help make your brand amazing and impossible to ignore.

Develop a Marketing Strategy

Marketability is what makes you compelling. Your goal is for others to be drawn in by your brand and want to invest in its success by giving you a job, venture capital, attention, or time. Think about what makes other brands marketable. Would you use a Nintendo Wii if it didn't let you interact with the screen or shop at Amazon.com if it didn't customize its interface to your preferences? The compelling nature of these companies drives us to their brands.

As you develop your brand marketing strategy, be sure to synchronize your personal value statement and brand differentiators into one powerful core message—and unleash it for your target audience. Remember, to communicate your brand message effectively, you need to believe in yourself and the brand you've established. You need to be confident and have the support of your core network. The attitude you convey is essential; if you don't believe in yourself, neither will your audience.

Six Qualities of a Successful Sales Pitch

Even if you don't think you're a salesperson, you should learn the following qualities of a successful sales pitch, because you will have to sell your brand to achieve your goals.

1: **Confidence.** The most important factor when engaging anyone, from influential executives to potential investors in your brand, is to have confidence in yourself and your abilities. You need to be confident in your personality, appearance, skills, and overall presentation and project this at all times.

2: **Preparation.** You should always be prepared to represent your brand; you never know when you will be placed in a situation that might be advantageous. To be prepared is to be ready for success at all times.

3: **Research.** Learn about your audience—whether it's a client, manager, or investor—before you even meet them. Google their name and try to learn who they are and how you should engage them. Your audience will be impressed if you can show you're aware of their achievements.

4: **Delivery.** To deliver a successful pitch, remember to say something concrete, important, and achievable.

5: **Speed.** Sometimes you are given very little time to deliver your pitch, so make the most of it. This means you have to be ready to unleash your best ideas quickly and get to the point.

6: **Follow-up.** Whether you succeed or fail with delivery, there is always opportunity for follow-up. Showing that you are interested in a person or the company is seen as positive.

Your audience has to embrace your brand for you to achieve your dreams. Think of an interview as you selling yourself (the product) to a hiring manager (audience)—if you've developed a convincing pitch, you will be a valuable and marketable brand.

Positioning Your Brand for Success

After you assess the key elements of your brand—your strong personal value statement, the things that differentiate you from everyone else, and your marketing strategy—you need to give them shape in the form of a development plan. This plan will give your brand a strategic framework, which you can employ as you share your brand with the world. Don't forget: it must be flexible, because the world around our brands is constantly changing.

Your Personal Brand Development Plan

Before you get started, it is helpful to define "personal success." If I were to define success from a personal branding standpoint, I would say that it is the ability to make money doing what I'm passionate about. Others may believe that you are successful if you raise a happy child, climb Mount Everest, or appear on a reality TV show. Some even define success as being a billionaire. I feel success is about owning your career, creating your salary, and being eager to go to work. Define what personal success means to you. This will help set your goals and develop a plan for achieving them.

" People should do what they do/love as well as they can. For me, it's blogging and speaking. My thinking is that if you do good stuff, your brand will naturally come out of your actions. But if you focus on 'what makes me look good,' you'll just be a slick and shallow persona. "

—Guy Kawasaki, managing director,
Garage Technology Ventures

When setting your goals, make sure you distinguish those that are short term from those that are long term. This will allow you to set a realistic time line for achieving each of them.

- **Short term.** These goals could have a time line anywhere from a few days to a few years, depending on your situation. For instance, if you want to be an accountant, your short-term goal might be to obtain your CPA or to get your master's degree in accounting in the next two years. If you want to develop networking relationships in your company's marketing department, then your short-term goal might be to attend marketing's "brown bag" lunch presentation on its new projects tomorrow.

- **Long term.** When you establish long-term goals, you are looking out into the future—where you would like to be in 5, 10, even 20 years. It's great to be optimistic and set the bar high, but you should also be realistic and consider your current situation as well.

By creating your goals, you are giving yourself something by which to measure success. Alignment between long-term and short-term goals is critical to their achievement. For instance, if you are determined to be a lawyer (long-term goal), you will need to go to law school, which means getting a high score on the LSAT (short-term goal). Your short-term goals should support your long-term dreams. Also, make your goals specific. "I want to be a millionaire," is not detailed enough. You really want to think about developing measurable goals.

Have SMART Goals

When defining your goals, make sure they are **SMART**: Specific, Measurable, Attainable, Realistic, and Timely.

Use the following sample development plan to help you define and refine the goals you have for brand YOU. Find a piece of paper, copy the chart in Figure 5.5, and fill out your own plan. Ideally, you want to build a plan that captures your current situation and carries you 15 years into the future. Think about where you are, where you want to be, and how to get there.

Figure 5.5. Sample Development Plan

Name: Dave Jordan
Age: 20
Occupation: Student at the University of Michigan

Life goals:
1) To be the leading authority in Web strategy consulting for small businesses
2) To be a respected and wealthy venture capitalist
3) To be happily married with two children and live in Los Angeles, California

Short-term goals:

6 months:
1) Research the Web strategy consulting field and take courses that will help me succeed in this field.
2) Purchase a new suit for professional networking.
3) Develop a professional blog and profiles on social networking sites.
4) Work on improving my confidence and verbal communication skills for interviews.
5) Get an internship in my chosen field.

1 year:
1) Complete a successful internship and get an entry-level job in Web consulting.
2) Meet key people through blogging and social networking.
3) Improve my Excel, PowerPoint, and HTML skills.

Long-term goals:

5 years:
1) Climb the corporate ladder in a respected Web development company.
2) Build management and leadership skills from executive-level management courses, mentorships, and work experience.
3) Continue to develop my brand through my website and blog and by attending various networking events.
4) Find a brand niche, maybe as a dynamic, young Web consultant expert who specializes in serving financial institutions.

15 years:
1) Become a manager with several employees under my leadership.
2) Work on establishing my own successful Web development company.
3) Seek out investment opportunities in other key business ventures.
4) Travel the world and speak to different colleges and companies about everything I've learned.
5) Meet a woman with a great sense of humor and with whom I share interests and values and start a family.

Keep in mind that your development plan is a constant work in progress—it will grow, deepen, and evolve as you change. After completing the first draft of your plan, you'll be ready to proceed with creating a powerful personal marketing plan.

Your Personal Marketing Plan

Any successful business has a business plan that includes marketing, operations, and finance sections. The purpose of a business plan is to build a case for starting a business and to attract potential stakeholders. A stakeholder could be an investor, a venture capital firm, or a business partner. Entrepreneurs can use a business plan to figure out the cost of doing business, analyze the market, and figure out how to gain a competitive advantage as they move forward.

A personal marketing plan is a strategic way for you to utilize your personal development plans toward achieving your career goals. Combined, these are the ultimate foundational tools for brand discovery and deployment. Remember, you can't construct a business—or a brand— without laying down the foundation.

Your personal marketing plan will require the following: a *situational analysis*, an *audience analysis*, a *personal SWOT analysis* (strengths, weaknesses, opportunities, and threats), a *competitive analysis*, a *marketing strategy*, and a *budgeting* and *action plan*. We'll discuss each of these below.

Situational Analysis

A situational analysis examines where you currently are in life (current situation), as well as your short- and long-term goals. Every brand needs a reason for being and a destination. A situational analysis will help you to develop the following key brand statements:

- **Mission Statement.** Your *mission statement* contains your personal value statement (what you offer) and how your audience (the people you want to impress to reach your long-term goals) can benefit by choosing your personal brand.

    Example: "I am a leader, team player, and strategist when it comes to actively recruiting and retaining employees with the end goal of building a talented pool of workers."

- **Vision Statement.** Where do you want to be in ten years? A *vision statement* describes what your brand is destined to be—if you put the work in. Many personal vision statements revolve around being a pioneer in a specific niche, while becoming recognized for personal and professional achievements.

    Example: "To be a world-recognized expert in the field of promoting and facilitating educational activities for college students who seek to make a positive impact on the world."

- **Value Statement.** Your values could be philanthropy, innovation, harmony, craftsmanship, or many others. In this area, you want to list what is true to you or what gives your brand meaning. The idea here is to discover what you believe in so you can best represent yourself.

> *Example:* "My values include community building and improving the environment."

- **Personal Brand Statement.** This is a single sentence that covers your areas of skill and mastery and who your target audience is. It should be factual and indicate clearly what you have to offer.

  > *Example:* "I'm the leading personal branding expert for Generation Y."

Audience Analysis

In business, a *market analysis* is a way to research and discover the market trends you're interested in pursuing. Your personal brand works in the same way, but your market is your *audience*. As you develop a brand that attracts an increasingly larger audience, more opportunities for success will open to you.

Build Your Audience!

Think of the power that blogs with large audiences wield; it's why Engadget, The Huffington Post, Boing Boing, and others are successful. Advertisers compensate based on size of audience, as measured by website visitors, fans, blog subscribers, people in your network, and potential customers interested in what you have to offer.

Your audience is who will come to your speaking events, email you for information, or want to do business with you, helping you to build brand credibility and reputation. Remember, audiences can be converted into friends, friends into clients, and clients into money. Get to know your target audience and work hard to give them what they want.

You'll want to find out where your audience lives, how they communicate, and what their lifestyle is like. If you're seeking a job, then research your prospective recruiters and companies; if your target audience is college students, you may want to pursue

Facebook. Be forewarned that with technology changing so fast, your audience will continue to change, and you will have to change as well to keep their attention. A successful brand today can be tossed away in a heartbeat if it isn't kept current and fresh. Audience analysis is an ongoing process; try adding a poll to your website or blog using the tools at *surveymonkey.com* or *polldaddy.com* to stay on top of the needs, wants, and desires of your audience.

Personal SWOT Analysis

When constructing a marketing plan, businesses of all sizes typically apply a SWOT analysis to see how they stand in relation to competitors.

A SWOT analysis involves examining your:

- strengths,
- weaknesses,
- opportunities, and
- threats.

Instead of doing a SWOT analysis for a product or competitor, let's focus it directly on your personal brand. As individuals, after all, we must direct our attention to maximizing our strengths, reducing our weaknesses, identifying opportunities, and stabilizing threats.

You might want to do an exercise where you brainstorm and write down how each of these areas pertains to your current situation. You can ask for feedback from others to deepen your analysis. Keep the following tips in mind:

- **Strengths.** Think of your most marketable skills, based on your specific goals and career aspirations. Is your ability to multitask your greatest strength, or is it your kinetic personality?
- **Weaknesses.** These are areas where you need improvement. They could range from your ability to speak or write effectively or your lack of technical savvy. Weak-

nesses are an important part of your development plan as well, and overcoming them should be among your goals.

- **Opportunities.** Throughout your career, you'll need opportunities to progress and gather new skills. Never miss out on an opportunity that fits into your development plan.

- **Threats.** Threats come in all shapes and sizes. A threat could be another individual competing for the same job, an environmental factor that may hinder your chances to succeed, or anything that could possibly make your brand irrelevant or outdated. Some threats can be avoided; others cannot. By building on your strengths and developing your weaknesses, you can anticipate and negate such threats.

Try filling out your own personal SWOT analysis in Figure 5.6. It's an invaluable exercise as you develop your brand.

Figure 5.6. My SWOT Analysis	
Strengths	**Weaknesses**
Opportunities	**Threats**

Competitive Analysis

After recognizing your audience's needs and what you can deliver, you need to assess your *competition*. Again, who your competition is will depend on your specific goals. If you're a doctor, lawyer, or dentist, you will most likely be competing based on location, reputation, and word-of-mouth referrals. If you're in college, you will be competing with other college graduates for entry-level positions in your chosen field.

When performing a competitive analysis for a prospective business, you should examine the top five to ten competitors in your niche and write down their product names, prices, differentiating characteristics, and features. Look into how they use technology, including websites, blogs, and networking sites, to their advantage. It's much more difficult to analyze the competition on a person-to-person basis, but if your brand is as powerful as it can possibly be, you may not have to worry much about the competition when searching for a job or trying to be the best in a particular field.

In today's increasingly wired world, new tools for performing competitive analysis appear constantly. Take websites and blogs, for example. Hundreds of websites monitor and rank other websites and blogs according to the number of hits per day they receive and user ratings. When you see websites and blogs that are rated higher than yours, it's a good idea to analyze them and try to determine why they are so successful. Then you can adjust your branding strategy accordingly.

Marketing Strategy

The foundation of marketing lies with the four **P**s: **p**roduct, **p**lace, **p**rice and **p**romotion. If you were to sell a new product, you would start by describing the following:

- The product itself
- Its convenience or accessibility
- Its low price or high value for the price
- Promotional tactics for attracting an audience

Applying the four **P**s to your personal brand will help you develop a powerful marketing strategy:

- **Person.** Instead of selling an object, you are selling your-self—*you* become the product.

- **Place.** *Place* is not only the location of companies for which you want to work; it is also the venues where you will network and meet new people. You will want to take the following factors into account when you make this choice: distance from your family and friends, accessibility, living conditions, nightlife, and more. The right place will yield an enriching experience that will also build your brand.

- **Price.** *Price* is your total net value. Often this is determined by the organizations that are in a position to consider hiring you as an employee. Your value encompasses your wealth of knowledge, title, skills, and experience that you bring to the table, along with any additional awards, accolades, and accomplishments you've amassed. As your value increases, you can demand more compensation and benefits from your employer. Ask yourself, "How much is Me Inc. worth?"

- **Promotion.** If you aren't detectable, then people won't know about you. Get your brand known through diligent *promotion*. You can promote yourself through speaking engagements; networking events; on blogs, websites, or social networks; or by any other means available to you. Creatively branding yourself will enhance your visibility and generate positive responses.

Once you research your audience, you need to segment it to find your niche and locate your target market. Your personal brand cannot please, nor is it relevant, to everyone walking this earth. Some people will value it, while others may be turned off. When determining your *target audience*, consider the following factors:

- Geographic
- Psychographic

- Demographic
- Behavioral

  Example: You want to target people who live in Manhattan who exercise three to five times per week, have a household income of at least $150,000, are between the ages of 28 and 40, and purchase your type of product ten times a year.

This example addresses each aspect of a target audience: geographic (Manhattan), psychographic (active lifestyle), demographic (household income and age range), and behavioral (purchasing occasion).

You don't always have to be that descriptive. You could say, "College students in New York who like to read often." The idea is to think about exactly whom you want in your audience and whom you don't. Sixty-year-olds don't want to read a college magazine, and a *Fortune* 500 company isn't going to hire someone with no work experience as a vice president. On both the corporate and individual level, one thing remains consistent—you need to research, observe, and direct your marketing messages at a specific target.

Budgeting and Action Plan

Regardless of the expense, when you budget for your personal brand, you want to keep a careful, itemized record including a description, the amount of the expense, and the date. Careful records are crucial for any budding business or brand.

If you're a new brand, then you probably need to budget frugally. Consider all options and make cost-effective decisions. For example, advertising is a common part of a brand's budget. You may pay for a ten-second spot on a TV or radio station or an advertisement in a local newspaper or company's catalog or on *Google AdWords* or Facebook. You'll want to choose the option that makes the most sense for your brand (that will reach your target audience).

Part of your budget may be your own blog or website, which requires the registration of a domain name; a hosting service; and graphic design, website development, and maintenance to make your online tools attractive to your audience. Again, allocate your resources based on your needs. If an eye-catching and highly interactive website is standard for your particular business or brand, spending the money needed to keep up with the competition may be a wise investment. Don't forget: the more knowledge and time you have, the less you have to pay others for these services. Why pay someone else to develop and maintain your website when you can learn to do it yourself?

A budget and strategy are useless unless you can execute them with an action plan. An action plan has several line items containing the title of the task, the time frame by which the task must be accomplished, and the cost. As you build your action plan, keep a checklist for completing necessary goals as you follow the development of your brand. Use the sample checklist in Figure 5.7 to help you develop your plans.

Figure 5.7. Sample Budget and Action Checklist

Task	Time Frame	Cost	Complete?
Purchase domain name	8/9/2009	$6.95	✓
Acquire logo	8/9 to 8/27/2009	$25.00	✓
Construct professional website	8/27 to 10/1/2009	$52.95	✓
Run Google AdWords	10/1 to 11/1 2009	$100.00	✓
Total Cost: $184.90			

Brand discovery is often a challenging process, yet it is rewarding. As you discover the key elements of your brand and shape them to achieve your goals, you will learn more about who you are and what you want out of your life. Although you have the option to shape and reshape your brand as you see fit, if you skip the brand discovery step, you may end up rebranding yourself more times than necessary, which can confuse and annoy your audience, not to mention creating a lot of work and frustration for you. Stay focused and remain committed to achieving the goals you have for your personal brand, and you can make your vision of a successful future a reality.

Chapter 6

Step 2—Create Your Brand

Creating a powerful personal brand requires the development of a killer online and offline presence that will grab hold of your target audience's attention—and refuse to let go! Showcasing brand *You* requires the ability to communicate its purpose and mission successfully, and to do so, you need powerful marketing tools working for you. These marketing tools make up your *personal branding toolkit*. This chapter will help you discover which tools are right for you as you build your own personal branding toolkit.

Online Brand Presence

For most personal brands, making an impact online is essential. This is especially true if you're looking to conquer the job recruitment process. In case you haven't noticed, the competition is tougher than ever, and brand *You* must truly stand out from the job-seeking herd to achieve your goals. It's time for you to start building your personal branding toolkit.

Your Personal Branding Toolkit

A successful personal branding toolkit is effective at any point in the corporate recruitment cycle. I will review some traditional tools that you should have, but I will also offer you strategies for bypassing traditional HR recruitment hurdles and proceeding directly to recruitment, including blogging and networking. Employing the entire toolkit will help your brand make an impact that prospective employers will notice.

Resume

The harsh truth is that most recruiters for major corporations spend 10 to 15 seconds examining each resume they receive (Beshara, 2006)[59]. This means that your resume must be a perfect representative of your brand and transmit your brand messaging succinctly and persuasively. You should keep your resume brief and concise, ensuring that it highlights the most important information—your experience, activities, and accomplishments.

Your resume should also include an objective and summary, especially if you're submitting it to a location that doesn't review cover letters. Also, there's no such thing as a "one-size-fits-all" resume. Each resume you create should be tailored to match the description of the job for which you're applying. When I crafted my resume, I purposely made it two pages to cover all my internship experience, technical skills, and leadership achievements. The sheer number of experiences I had was part of my value proposition and differentiation strategy. Resumes should tell a story—about how you and your abilities and experience are a perfect match for the position.

Key items to include in your first professional resume include these:

- **Objective.** Your short- and long-term goals and what you want to get out of the job for which you're applying

- **Summary.** A brief "elevator pitch" (it could be delivered during an elevator ride) introducing you to whoever's reading your resume

- **Education.** A list of your relevant degrees, courses, GPA, and any scholastic honors you've amassed, such as being on the dean's list

- **Technical skills.** A summary of your technical know-how, including I/T certifications and software packages you can use

- **Work experience.** Starting from the most recent experience (either an internship or full-time job), a summary using at least three bullet points to describe each experience. Use appropriate action words and dynamic language to punch things up, and be sure to include any on-the-job accomplishments.

- **Extracurricular activities.** A list of all the organizations, groups, and clubs you've been a part of, including your specific roles in each.

As you gain more job experience after college, tighten up your resume. Instead of listing extracurricular activities, you should list the various associations of which you are a member and remove your relevant college courses from the education section, leaving just the degrees and honors. Then expand the experience section to include all of your jobs. List your major projects with results and a summary of your skills. As you progress in your career, the experience section will become the most important part of your resume.

Cutting-Edge Resume Tools: LinkedIn and Video

As previously mentioned, using the Internet and modern technology—in an appropriate and professional manner—can help you stand out during your job search. Having a profile on LinkedIn and creating a video resume are two great ways of doing so.

- **LinkedIn Tips.** I recommend registering for LinkedIn (*linkedin.com*); your profile will be optimized and made visible to recruiters through searches within the application. It will also show up in Google searches, where LinkedIn profiles enjoy a high status. Always keep your profile up to date, accurate, and linked to your other websites or blogs. The best LinkedIn profiles have powerful written endorsements, a catchy headline, and a strong summary paragraph.

- **Video Resume Tips.** A video resume is a great way to showcase your entire brand, including your personality, appearance, and mannerisms. Make sure you don't read from a script; your words should come naturally. You should limit the session to only a few minutes and communicate your core message confidently. Try to articulate clearly what would normally be found in a written resume but with energy. If done correctly, a video resume can make a powerful, personal impact.

Cover Letter

This letter should detail your reason for wanting to work for your target company. Most companies now require this document as a way of proving that you're serious about the position. It should focus on how you fit the job qualifications and provide a summary of your background. This should be a formal letter that includes the company's name, address, and the contact's name if known. It should be clear and have a strong, positive impact on the reader, but it should not employ any unnecessary bells and whistles— adding a photo of your dog or a clever poem you wrote won't score you any points.

References Document

Although this document is not a requirement, if you were interviewing someone, wouldn't you be impressed by a list of professional references? When compiling this document, keep in mind that it must be clear and provide information that a recruiter can use to conduct a background check. You should list three to five trusted contacts, from your previous employers to college professors and supervisors at places you've volunteered with. It should be formatted in the center of the page, with the company's name in bold, followed by the contact's name, title, phone number, and email address.

Portfolio (CD/Print/Website)

For many industries, a portfolio, whether in print, on a CD, or on your website, is mandatory. Graphic designers, photographers, animators, and others must prove their competence through their previous work. Writers should provide writing samples and clips for journalists. Consider your portfolio review as an opportunity to display your best work to interviewers. It lets them know that you're serious and motivated. Remember to include only your most relevant and professional work for the position—reviewers won't have much time to review submission materials, so like your resume, it should clearly display your brand value.

When I was interviewing for my first job, I burned a CD of all my prior work and even customized the CD cover. My portfolio had a slideshow of the various websites I had created, as well as snapshots of my experiences at previous corporations. It really added to my credibility and value. Of course, a CD isn't the only acceptable format. You can always print samples of your work or display your work on your website.

Interviewing Skills

Effective interviewing skills are a powerful part of your toolkit. They're essential to achieving your career goals—you have to get your foot in the door before you can show a potential employer what you have to offer.

When approaching an interview, students and professionals tend to ask many questions. How should I dress? What should I say and bring? How should I follow up? Is this job the best fit for me? Would it be worth relocating if I get an offer?

My advice is to be ready for anything. During an interview, it's a safe bet you'll be asked a mix of traditional and unorthodox questions. Make sure you're professional, polished, and confident and that your verbal and body language are communicating your brand positively. The chart in Figure 6.1 summarizes my advice for handling some common interview questions.

Figure 6.1. Common Interview Questions

Question	How to Respond
How would you describe yourself?	• List your top brand attributes. Examples may include determined, energetic, intelligent, insightful, outgoing, and being a team player.
What do you know about this organization?	• Before interviewing, research the organization. • Learn about the executive management team, as well as the products and services sold. Being aware of any specific milestone dates and interesting facts will make you look good.
What are your long-range goals and objectives?	• Include the company where you're interviewing as part of your goals. • Employers want to hear how you can align both short- and long-term goals and that their organization is part of your plan.
What are your strengths, weaknesses, and interests?	• Although people detest mentioning weaknesses, we aren't perfect; speaking to your weaknesses and how you will overcome them will help you. • Listing your interests and strengths—and how they play off each other—is also beneficial.
How do you think a friend or colleague who knows you well would describe you?	• Be truthful and mention an instance when you received positive feedback from someone.

Question	How to Respond
Describe a situation in which you had to work with a difficult person. How did you handle the situation? Is there anything you would have done differently in hindsight?	• If possible, name a specific project where you had a management role and had to change your leadership tactics to adjust to difficulty. • Even if you couldn't accommodate the difficult team member, explain how you were able to manage the rest of the team despite that one group member. • Teamwork is essential in organizations, so shine a light on your project management and team participation skills.
In what ways do you think you can make a contribution to our organization?	• Match your personal value to your prospective employer's needs. If the organization is looking for someone to develop its website, you will want to mention your coding ability, as well as showing samples of your best design work.

Beyond focusing on what you can offer a prospective employer, you should think about what the job can offer you. Take the time to ask yourself the following: "Does this job match my brand?" Think about how you will profit from a possible job offer, including compensation, benefits, and the value of the work experience. If you feel that the job will serve as a stepping-stone or you would like to have a long-term career there, then it may be a good fit for your brand. If you're not sure, proceed carefully. Be cautious: don't get sidetracked on your road to success!

A Website—Your eBrand Framework

After creating a resume, portfolio, video, and LinkedIn profile, you are ready to build your personal eBrand. Your personal *eBrand* is your online presence, a digital representation of you on the Internet. In today's world, it's hard to survive without a strong presence on the Internet, and having your own website is becoming increasingly more important.

Before getting started, you should understand some of your options for creating your website:

- **Option 1: Be the programmer.** If you have the necessary technical skills, including graphic design and HTML know-how, or can operate software packages such as Microsoft Expression Web or Macromedia Dreamweaver, you can get started right away. Learning these skills will benefit you in the long run, letting you save money and giving you more control over your Internet image. You can teach yourself, take a class, or learn from an online training course from the convenience of your home.

- **Option 2: Use basic tools.** Many hosting platforms cater to those without much technical background. They offer site builders, which allow you to choose premade templates. Many sites offer free Web space in exchange for hosting advertisements on your pages; others give you the option to purchase space at a low cost. Buying your own space gives you a free domain and more flexibility with the amount of file storage and bandwidth. Weebly (*weebly.com*), Bravenet (*bravenet.com*), Google pages (*pages.google.com*), and MySite (*mysite.com*) offer free services you can use. 1&1 (*order.1and1.com*), HostMonster (*hostmonster.com*), and *GoDaddy.com* are three of the top hosting services to use with a paid subscription; these offer maximum space and options that help you get started right away. If you purchase hosting from one of these services, your domain registration is free. If you've already bought *YourName.com*, you can purchase hosting and use that name as well.

- **Option 3: Hire an expert.** If you aren't proficient with the Web and don't have someone in your network who can assist you, you can outsource this project. Keep in mind that this option might cause you to lose some creative control, and you'll have to pay for ongoing maintenance to the website. Depending on your objective and the consultant you hire, this operation can run you anywhere from $500 to $5,000 or more. Remember, you get what you pay for in any transaction.

Many website menu section options are available. Some will be more relevant to you than others, so choose wisely. Options include these:

- Bio
- Blog
- Career highlights
- Contact
- Endorsements
- Experience
- News and events

- Photos
- Portfolio and sample projects
- Press/media
- Skills
- Social networks
- Videos

Take your sections and spread them across your homepage—and make navigating your site (finding information on it) user-friendly. When someone clicks on one of your sections, the content matching that section should appear. For instance, if you click on a "career highlights" section, the area should clearly list your highlights. Congratulations: By doing this, you have now set-up your site navigation!

After setting up your website, implement its design wherever

eBranding Tips

Consider these ebranding tips when building your website:

- **Always** include your name, picture, and personal brand statement.
- **Always** include personal information, not just professional experience, so that the user can get a feeling for your ebrand. Revealing a little about yourself will help you establish an

emotional connection with the audience. (Obviously, you don't want to reveal anything that could jeopardize your safety.)

- **Always** keep your site engaging, user-friendly, and easy to navigate.

- **Always** use aesthetic choices (font style, background color, logos, etc.) that will capture and hold your audience's attention without annoying them. Visitors to your website will make a quick decision based on what they see, so it needs to make a great first impression.

- **Always** use design choices, including a color scheme, that represents your personal brand. You can use the products at *colorschemer.com* to help you choose your scheme.

possible, such as on your resume and business card. Everything you make from this point forward should reflect a consistent brand feel.

In addition, consider making other tools in your personal branding toolkit, including your resume, portfolio, and video resume, available on your website. You can also link to your social networking pages or include your blog feed on the site. This incorporation will tie everything together and give you an integrated "face" to show the world. And remember to keep things up to date; as you garner new personal achievements, projects, or proud moments over the life span of your eBrand, update your website to showcase them.

Blogs

Your website is a great starting point for building your online presence, but it isn't the only tool available. Blogs provide new channels of communications and are great self-promotion platforms—perfect for building your personal brand.

" Blogs allow anyone with bright ideas and interesting perspectives to be found and heard. Blogs are personal, direct, and unsanitized by marketing people. Blogs enable a personal conversation with the people directly involved in making it happen. **"**

—Don Dodge, director of business development, Microsoft

The Power of the Blogosphere: A Case Study

Blogs were instrumental in the development of my individual brand, and by sharing my early blog experiences, I hope to show that anyone can harness the power of the blog for personal branding success.

My "Personal Branding Blog" started off as a repository of my previous blog's content, just in a new structure. When developing my first blog logo, the general concept was "Navigating you to future success." I was able to use my Web development and graphic design skills, which I had acquired during high school. I designed a 3D logo of a black silhouette inside a compass. The compass represented the knowledge others would gather from reading my blog material as I pointed them in the right direction for their careers.

I discovered that *Wordpress.com*, the zenith of blog-hosting websites, offered many templates for blogs, as well as custom headings and a sleek commenting system. It also featured *widgets*, small Web contraptions that display a specific type of content (graphic, video, etc.) or applications that can be embedded on a blog or other Web page. The chart in Figure 6.2 highlights some of the current pros and cons of the more popular blog-hosting sites.

Figure 6.2. Blog Hosting Options

Wordpress.com	TypePad.com
• Membership is free and you get your own URL— **website.wordpress.com.** • With this site you have spam protection from Akismet. • Wordpress ranks high in Google and there is a support forum for the product. • There are certain limitations—you can't edit the site's overall structure, you are not permitted to use JavaScript, and you can't add plug-ins.	• It costs $49.95 for the year for a personal blog and you receive a URL— **website.typepad.com.** • If you want to use your own domain name, it costs $89.95 annually. • This host is spam protected, contains various design templates, and integrates your social networks. • You can invite guest-bloggers to your blog who are already members of the TypePad community.
WordPress	**Movable Type**
• You can download the client at **wordpress.org** and host it somewhere else. • After purchasing your domain and space on this system, you can upload the WordPress template you choose to the server via FTP (file transfer protocol, a way to move files between your computer and the Internet). • You can load new plug-ins (applications with extra functionality) within your blog and are not subject to the boundaries that WordPress presents.	• You can download this platform for free from **movabletype.org** and upload it to a host, which will charge hosting fees. • Much as with WordPress, you have a great deal of control over the layout, design, and technical aspects of your blogging experience.
Blogger	**Tumblr**
• Blogger (**www.blogger.com**) is a free hosting service run by Google. • It offers a few templates, and getting started is quite easy. • You can only use JavaScript and HTML, and there are very few customization options to fit your brand. • The comments section of each blog post opens up a new window, making navigating less user-friendly than it might be.	• Tumblr (**tumblr.com**)is a personal "life-streaming" service, which is a record of your daily activities on all social networks. • This type of format is more about short-form, mixed-media posts rather than full-blown blog posts.

My "Personal Branding Blog" had limited traffic during the first few weeks of its existence. To solve this issue, I used Technorati and Google Blog Search to search for key words, such as *marketing*, *branding*, *personal branding*, and *social media*. I was interested in finding sites that would have relevance to my blog theme, heavy traffic, a high PageRank™, a loyal community, and a 200+ Technorati authority, meaning that hundreds of other blogs linked to them. I started to reach out, both on-blog and off-blog, to many influencers.

I would comment on various posts on-blog and then follow-up with an email to the author off-blog. It's just like if you went on an interview (on-blog) and then sent the interviewer a short email (off-blog) thanking him for his time. Commenting was my way of interacting with others who wrote about personal branding and related topics. I noticed that after leaving a comment, the blog owner would subscribe to my blog and comment on my posts. As each new visitor was morphed into a subscriber, the blog formed into a community.

I learned that there were approximately five blogs on the topic of personal branding when I started, but there were absolutely no representatives from Gen Y blogging in this space. Remember when we discussed *market niches* in chapter 5? I seized the opportunity and differentiated my new personal brand to occupy this niche.

I was well aware that people were recording themselves and uploading the *podcasts* to YouTube, but I had never thought about replicating this exercise in my blog. I soon realized that personal branding through video was a great way to showcase my brand. I purchased a Web camera and video-editing software and challenged myself to learn podcasting. Soon after, I launched "Personal Branding TV." I uploaded my video episodes to YouTube and posted them as blog entries. I got mixed responses from my community; the feedback I received, both positive and negative, really helped me to refine my work. Before long, Personal Branding TV became an anticipated show on my blog.

I quickly grew eager to promote my brands through other available media outlets. Since I was already Web writing for magazines, I figured that publishing my own magazine would be a worthwhile venture. I used both my existing graphic design skills and my online community to get things moving. I knew I could craft an artistic cover, and I had a thorough comprehension of layout, placement, and promotion. I recognized that the community I'd built with my blog could serve as contributors to the magazine.

My blog community even helped sponsor the first issue. In addition, I could distribute and promote the magazine through a website that allowed users to purchase a subscription. I had a very limited budget at this time, but the contributors were more than happy to promote the magazine on their blogs, with the hope that positive word-of-mouth would travel virally across the blogosphere. My passion, as well as that of the contributors', powered the magazine. The Internet gave me the reach needed to pull knowledge from around the world and showcase a full perspective on personal branding.

While I was blogging and promoting my brand, I was also developing new brand goals. My goal was to formulate a website that would be the ultimate personal brand consortium. *DanSchawbel.com* was a cross between my personal and professional life, integrated with social media, and it contained all things related to my personal brand—endorsements, press clippings, and workshop podcasts, as well as my skills, brand attributes, and hobbies.

The site was the ultimate culmination of my personal brand. I built it not only for myself but to show the world that anyone can do it. No matter which technologies or ideas I employed, the blogosphere served as the hub of operations for developing my personal brand—and it can do the same for you!

How You Can Start a Blog

Starting a blog is simple—start blogging. The only true way to learn about blogging is to get involved. I started off without any knowledge, but the more I tested out strategies, the more quickly I learned what was successful and what wasn't.

Your Blog Strategy

When choosing a strategy for your blog, ask yourself the following:

- Will you keep a live journal of your personal thoughts and share them with your friends?

- Will you start a blog for your business or your personal brand?

- What media types are you planning on using (e.g., video, pictures)?

- Whom do you want to access the blog to read/download the content? To create/upload content?

After determining your blogging strategy, follow these steps to build your own successful blog:

1: **Listen to conversations.** Before you choose a niche, pay attention to what's already out there. See what new ideas you can add. This will help you to differentiate your blog from the rest. The best way to accomplish this is to get a *feed reader*, which sends updates from the blogs you select directly to you, and subscribe to blogs.

There are many readers out there, but I recommend Google's because it allows you to categorize your feeds, view trends, and check entries that get your attention. Other popular services include Bloglines and Newsgator. Subscribe to blogs that touch on your topic, as well as blogs that are outside your comfort zone, so you can expand your knowledge and offer your readers more value.

2: Niche positioning. Unless you're already a world-renowned and respected brand, you should narrow your blog to focus on a specific niche. Having a niche will help you become an expert in an area where there are fewer competitors. Remember, your brand can't serve everyone.

3: YourName.com. Take a quick break from reading this book and register *YourName.com* at the hosting site of your choice. If you have a common name, you will have to include your middle name or a nickname in your domain name. Getting your own domain for your blog and/or personal website is relatively inexpensive, and it's a great first step toward building your own powerful brand.

4: Choose your platform. There are lots of options to use as your blog's platform. Some cost money; others are free. Most of them come with free templates that can help you get started immediately.

5: Logo and theme. Your blog's logo and theme should reflect your unique brand concept. After you register your blog, you'll be given sample themes to choose from, but you must supply your own logo. Whether you hire a graphic artist or design your own logo, choose carefully—remember that people connect from an experience to a logo to a brand.

6: "About" page. Believe it or not, the most viewed page on my blog is not a post; it's my "About" page. Visitors will almost always pay attention to your "About" page to size up your writing by getting to know your brand. If your brand doesn't inspire confidence or credibility, visitors will be turned off. The more credibility you build up in your "About" section, the more people will take the time to view your entries.

7: Blog subscription. One of your blogging goals should be to convert visitors into regular readers. Your subscription link, either to *Feedburner* or *FeedBlitz*, should be included as a widget on your sidebar (a part of your

Web page off to one side that has accessories and links rather than primary content). Feedburner (*feedburner.com*; recently acquired by Google) is a feed reader subscription service. FeedBlitz (*feedblitz.com*)is an email subscription service that will email each post that you publish on your blog to anyone who signs up.

You want to give your visitors many channels to receive information, as they have a variety of preferences. Post a link to your feed at the end of each post and include it in your email signature.

8: **Register your blog.** Every blog should be registered with Technorati (*technorati.com*) because that's how bloggers search and locate new blogs. Upon arrival, you will have to create a profile with your avatar, site title, URL and description. Make sure everything you enter matches the terms you use on your blog platform.

Posting on Your Blog

Now that you have a blog, you need to fill it with content. From my experience in the blogosphere, content is valued more than design. Think about it: How are you supposed to meet someone and maintain a conversation if there is nothing to talk about? Ensure that your content is appealing, original, informed, and open for comments. The best blogs are the ones that have access to information others do not.

Writing entries once a month just won't cut it. You need to post frequently, between two and five times per week, so that you are viewed as an active contributor of your community and people can rely on you for information. If you line up a series of posts on a given topic, it will help you post more frequently and serve as an indicator to your readers that another post is coming soon.

Here are some tips for writing a killer blog post:

- **Headlines are critical.** When your blog entry comes up in someone's feed reader, that person will immediately look at the title, and if it doesn't interest her, she'll move on. Your titles need to be catchy, controversial, or insightful. Many blogs use top-ten lists and provide *value-transparent* titles (where the value of reading the whole post is obvious) such as "Five Steps to Build a Better Blog."

- **Write as yourself.** Personal branding is about being authentic and transparent online, which means you should be honest and open and write as you would speak in reality. People appreciate this and will respond by paying attention and commenting.

- **Be informed and opinionated.** You need to have your own informed point of view on a topic if you want to be viewed as an expert. Stating your valued opinions will draw in more readers and keep the conversation lively.

- **Use multimedia.** Do not write a post without at least inserting one illustration that goes along with what you write. People prefer to visualize while reading online, and the more creative you can be, the better. Video podcasts will further differentiate your posts.

- **Be concise.** Try not to write more than 250 words for each blog post. People don't have time to go through long essays, especially when the majority of bloggers subscribe to upwards of 100 blogs at a time.

- **Use formatting.** You should include subtitles and bulleted lists when possible and use bold, italics, and underlining for key words and phrases to make each post an easier read.

- **Use key words.** Each blog post you write should use certain key words. When someone searches for your information on Google, what words will he use? Use those key words multiple times in your posts to have a good chance at ranking high for those search terms.

- **Link to other blogs.** Within your posts, you have the ability to link to other blogs. Choose words that a reader would like to understand more about and link them to a blog that can clarify that subject. You can link to others through a specific key word that represents them, a complete blog post about them, a guest post, or a listing of top blogs. Focus your efforts on blogs with more traffic and higher rankings, so you earn their respect and boost your readership and credibility.

How to Market Your Blog

So now you have a great blog and some awesome posts. What can you do to get the word out across the blogosphere? Use the following guidelines for marketing your blog and getting the word out about your killer personal brand:

- **Comments.** There's no better way to attract new readers, brand yourself on other blogs, and network than commenting. It is also a way of demonstrating genuine interest in other people, developing your interpersonal communication skills, and building your network. By commenting on other blogs, you're helping to promote topics that matter to you and keep them active. When others comment on your posts, comment back.

- **Widgets.** To differentiate your blog from the millions of others, you must use widgets. Widgets are stored on the sidebars of your blog, which are the areas that remain constant as you scroll down each blog entry. The most popular widgets at your disposal are a calendar, advertisements such as those from Google AdWords, a favorite book list, blog subscription *chicklets* (small icons) to indicate the availability of any RSS feeds, social networking utilities, a *tag cloud* (a list of key words that a reader can click to get to related posts on your blog), a search option, a hit counter, and contact options. Widgets demonstrate blog and Web competency.

- **Blogroll.** The most crucial widget is a *blogroll*, which is a list of links to your favorite blogs. Adding links to this list will not only help your readers, it will act as a networking device. Reach out to other bloggers and exchange links on your blogrolls and you will mutually benefit. Develop your blogroll to boost your site's popularity on search engines, while gaining the respect of other blog readers who will notice your link.

- **Guest posting.** One of the latest and greatest blog strategies is to write guest blog posts for other blogs, tailored to their readership. By guest posting, you are helping others by providing valuable content, as well as gaining visibility among the readers of another blog—hopefully directing traffic to your blog. You can write or accept guest posts for your own blog and benefit from having new content and flavor. Once your credibility and expertise on a certain topic becomes known, you can even earn some money by guest posting.

- **Entertainment.** Choose a game or contest that applies to your topic to engage your readers. I chose "Brand Mystery," where I placed a fuzzy picture of a celebrity brand and asked the community to guess who it was. The winners got their names and links to their websites in the next post. Many bloggers also run contests, where they award correct answers to quiz questions with promotional goods like T-shirts.

- **Signatures on email/forums.** Take your blog or feed URL and use it as part of your email and discussion forum signature along with your name, personal brand statement, and preferred method of contact.

- **Interviews.** Who wouldn't want to be interviewed? One of the best ways to network is by interviewing someone successful and interesting for your blog. All you have to do is email them no more than ten questions and have her send you back the written answers. Copy and paste what you receive and wrap it up in a blog post, linking to their website.

- **Social networks.** In general, by establishing profiles on social networks, you promote your blog as an application or within your profile information.

Anyone on earth can have a blog. Marc Cuban (*blogmaverick.com*), the owner of the NBA Dollar Mavericks team, has one. Heck, even MC Hammer (*mchammer.blogspot.com*) has a blog! Lots of other celebrities have blogs as a way to reach out and interact with fans, who would not usually be able to comment or connect personally through regular fan mail. You don't have to be a Web developer to understand how to blog or an artist to do the graphic design. All you need is time, ambition, and ideas. Studies show that blogging can help your social life, making you feel less isolated and more connected, both online and off.

Use the blog success checklist in Figure 6.3 to ensure that you're making the most of your time in the blogosphere.

	Figure 6.3. Blog Success Checklist	
1.	Get a feed reader and subscribe to ten blogs.	☐
2.	Determine your niche.	☐
3.	Register *YourName.com.*	☐
4.	Select a platform.	☐
5.	Choose a logo and theme.	☐
6.	Create an "About" page.	☐
7.	Add an RSS subscription link to your blog.	☐
8.	Register your blog at *Technorati.com.*	☐
9.	Add a blogroll widget and link at least five of your favorite blogs.	☐
10.	Write at least five blog posts before you publish them.	☐
11.	Guest-post on another blog.	☐

12.	Start a game or contest with your community.	☐
13.	Podcast yourself, others, or an event.	☐
14.	Write an article for a popular online resource, link it back to your blog, and promote it as a post within your blog.	☐
15.	Join two or three social networks and add your blog's URL to your profiles.	☐
16.	Add your blog's URL to your email signature.	☐
17.	Join one or more online discussion forums and add your blog's URL to your signature.	☐
18.	Interview your favorite blogger.	☐

Podcast Your Brand

Podcasting is a great tool for clearly expressing your brand. Video is a way to show your brand through words and visuals. It also allows your readers to match who you are online with your off-line identity. Podcasting is mainstream now and is used by regular folks and celebrities alike. Even P. Diddy has used the medium to hold a contest, asking for videos of people who want to be his next personal assistant. YouTube is the most widely known service for video sharing, but several others exist.

To set up a podcast, you need a few key pieces of equipment:

- **Digital video camera or webcam.** These can cost between $100 and $1,000 or more, depending on the quality of lens, memory size, and zoom features.

- **Microphone.** If you're passionate about podcasting or want to start a podcast business, a microphone is essential. A good microphone can cost between $20 and $200 or more, depending on your needs. A microphone is great for podcast interviews, especially during events where there is noise in the background.

- **Editing software.** Because not every podcast is perfect, video-editing software will help you create custom podcasts, add graphics and animations over video, and remove unwanted clips.

Online Social Networking Sites

Social networks are websites that connect people virtually. In this day and age, if you aren't active on social networks, you are in danger of being "out of the loop." Social networks are wonderful tools that can reinforce your brand and allow you to make valuable contacts, share information, and extend your brand's reach. Many individuals enter into these networks without bearing personal branding in mind; they miss out on key opportunities. To make effective use of social networking, you will want to do some careful planning and preparation.

> **The greatest tool I've used to grow my personal brand is social networking....Since I'm using my real name, and not some kind of cute handle (nickname), when someone sees me on TV or at a conference, they make the association with my online presence much more quickly.**
>
> —Veronica Belmont, host and producer, Revision3

Start with an Avatar

A picture is worth more than 1,000 words because it separates you from everyone else in the world (except maybe a twin). *Avatars* are small photographs that are used to showcase your identity on social networks. Creating an avatar is as easy as taking your picture, using an image editor (free on many computers out of the box) to condense it into an image that is 128 × 128 pixels in size, and putting it on your computer. Avatars are also used to verify who is commenting on a specific blog and are key aspects of your personal brand's online presence.

The best practice for using avatars is to spread the same picture across all social networks, whether blogs, websites, or pieces of freelance writing. Many people on the Web have avatars of clowns, objects, cartoons, and even Homer Simpson, all of which are ways of expressing yourself in a humorous manner but are poor for professional personal branding. Your self-portrait is what you need to use to help people associate your writing and presence with your brand.

Craft a Consistent Profile

Most social networks share similar profile input fields. By listing these fields and filling them in before you join networks, your profiles will be consistent, and you'll be one step ahead of the game. These are the most common fields:

- **Name.** Your most important asset. As you join social networks, your name should be spread consistently across all of them. The more times people see your name on various networks, the more it will resonate.

- **Headline.** A quick one- to three-word personal introduction. Choose your words carefully.

- **Summary.** A personal summary, captured in a single paragraph. Make it count.

- **Education.** The schools you've attended, your academic achievements, and the extracurricular activities you've taken part in.

- **Work.** The companies you've worked for or interned with. Highlight your work achievements and skills if possible.

- **Pictures.** All social networks request your picture to identify who you are. You also have the option of adding and tagging a series of pictures on select networks. Make sure your pictures represent your brand well.

- **Website.** Only a portion of your brand can be captured within your profile page, so lure interested parties to your blog or website to promote your brand.

- **Interests.** Most networks allow you to list your hobbies, as well as favorite TV shows, movies, and music. Tailor your interests to showcase your brand.

Dealing with Network Overload

The sheer number of social networks is nearly overwhelming. Which ones should you join? Which ones should you avoid? Should you join all of them? These are important questions to consider when developing a strategy for promoting your brand.

We all lead busy lives and have only a certain amount of time each day to dedicate to social networks. The more social networks you join, the more you must perform routine maintenance on each profile to keep it current. That can be a lot of work!

Before registering and participating in a social network, perform a three-part assessment:

1: Relevancy. First ask yourself, "How relevant is this network to my current situation?" If you have a rock band, then a profile on MySpace showcasing your latest hits would be relevant to your needs and audience. Totspot (*totspot.com*) targets new mothers who create profiles for themselves and their babies and add other mothers or kids as friends—if you're a single male, this is probably not the right destination for your brand. Eons (*eons.com*), a social networking site for baby boomers, might not be the best resource for Gen Y professionals.

2: Volume. Research the total volume or user base of the network. Any network is only as strong as the number of people with whom you can connect and communicate. A few thousand registered users might not be substantial enough to justify joining a social network—unless it's targeted to a very specific audience with which you are trying to connect.

3: Credibility. Figure out how credible and exclusive the membership is. You will want to stay away from networks with a few million registered users who are inactive, unless the network is very relevant to your situation and brand goals. The more credible the members are, the more likely your brand will benefit from joining. For instance, Michael Dell is on Facebook and Bill Gates has a LinkedIn account.

My advice is to join the most innovative networks with the largest installed user base. There are millions of users on the most popular social networks; other social networks have a fraction of this number, and few provide strong differentiation. In general, if you can't pinpoint a reason to join one of the latter kind of networks, then don't join it.

Your social network accounts should be connected to your blog, website, or your profiles at other networks to integrate your brand. Think of each as a piece of a puzzle: when put together, the entire picture—your brand—becomes clear!

The table in Figure 6.4 highlights the most popular social networking sites out there. Keep in mind that on the Internet, things change fast. A site may be hot today only to be forgotten tomorrow. Also, the key features of each site change all the time. My advice is to do your research and try to stay on top of the latest Internet happenings.

Figure 6.4. Popular Social Networking Sites		
Name	**Type**	**Description**
Facebook	Social community	• Facebook is currently the dominant social network, giving you free access to a variety of events, groups, and profile pages from around the world. • Facebook's audience were once college students but has since gravitated toward businesses, allowing users to fuse their personal and professional lives together.

Figure 6.4. Popular Social Networking Sites, continued

Facebook, continued	Social community	• Remember to set privacy controls, as it is an open platform where your coworkers as well as your friends can access your information.
MySpace	Social community	• MySpace's audience leans more to musicians, Hollywood celebrities like Paris Hilton, and a million or so fake spam profiles. • Like Facebook, you will want to set strict privacy controls and constantly monitor your account for strange activity.
MyBlogLog	Social community	• Many blogs are powered with MyBlogLog widgets, which showcase avatars of your recent visitors. • To unlock the full potential of this social network, add friends and follow up with your visitors once you identify them by their avatars. • As people join your blog network, you can even notify them of newly created blog posts or major events through the MyBlogLog messaging system.
Ning	Social community	• Launch, invite, and facilitate your own free social network in minutes. • Your network can be on the topic of your choice, and everyone who joins it will perceive you as the authoritative leader of the network.
LinkedIn	Professional network	• This network was built for users to make professional contacts. • As your friends and colleagues develop in their careers, LinkedIn allows you to follow their path with updates. • LinkedIn acts as a virtual resume and venue for expressing your personal brand.
YouTube	Video	• This is the number one video-sharing site on the Internet. • Aside from the parameters it gives you on file size (1 gigabyte) and length (less than ten minutes), it's a great place for podcasts, video resumes, or for creating a viral video that can stimulate traffic to your website.

Figure 6.4. Popular Social Networking Sites, continued

Viddler	Video	• The difference between Viddler and YouTube is that with Viddler, you can upload only 500 megabytes. • A big plus is that your videos can be over ten minutes long.
Flickr	Photos	• Flickr is a photo-sharing website where you can tag pictures of your friends, store them, and use them in your website or blog. • You can even arrange the pictures in various categories and display them to your liking.
Del.icio.us	Bookmarking	• As you browse the Web, you will land on sites that serve as training modules or areas of interest to you. Del.icio.us will help you bookmark and organize these sites. • You can even use a Del.icio.us widget on your blog so that your readers can add your posts to their Del.icio.us page. • AddThis (addthis.com) offers a widget for your visitors to add your blog to any social bookmarking website.
Digg	Bookmarking	• Submit and rate news content to increase the traffic to your blog posts. • Digg users have full control over what content makes the homepage, so be clever when it comes to the title of your submission. • There are also plug-ins that you can integrate into your blog so that your readers can submit posts for you.
StumbleUpon	Bookmarking	• Discover and share content from any site on the Internet and make recommendations to the rest of the network. • By downloading StumbleUpon's toolbar, you can submit your rating for the websites you visit. • You can also give your blog a StumbleUpon plug-in so that your community can rate your posts and share them.

Figure 6.4. Popular Social Networking Sites, continued		
Twitter	Microblogging	• Broadcast your current activities or thoughts, either by typing or using your phone to text up to 140 characters per message. • Twitter distributes your message to everyone who is following your account name and allows you to get updates as your friends send messages as well. • This is a great way to notify your network of changes in your life or what you're currently pondering. • It's also great for networking because you can use the "@" symbol, followed by an account name, and send direct messages to others.
FriendFeed	Social aggregation	• FriendFeed takes all the updates from your social websites, including every blog post you publish and YouTube video you mark as a favorite, and syndicates them on a single page. • People can follow your account and be notified of every update, and you can post your own FriendFeed updates on your page.

Social networks are part of our culture now and will soon be part of larger global movements. Of college students, 75 percent are participating in social networks (Anderson Analytics, 2007)[60], and this figure is predicated to rise to 84 percent by 2011. Also by 2011, 50 percent of online adults will be active in social networking platforms (eMarketer, 2007)[61]. Before long, when meeting others, fewer people will ask you for your phone number or email address; more frequently, they will either Google your name or add you as a friend in a social network.

If you aren't actively involved in social networks, you will be at a competitive disadvantage in both being recruited professionally and interfacing with your friends, family, fellow employees, and potential key contacts. Take social networking seriously and use it to your brand's advantage!

149

Creating your *personal e-Brand* is a necessity in a world driven by technology. An ebrand, as transparent and astonishing as it may be, is only an extension of your offline brand. As you pursue real-life situations, don't forget to pack your personality, appearance, and overall value into your online identity. A strong ebrand is harmonized by an offline brand that shares the same attributes, but can also remain consistent and relevant to your audience.

Portable Branding

Online branding will continue to grow more portable. Portability will come in the form of cell phones, PDAs, and products like Amazon's Kindle (an electronic reading product). Jobfox offers the ability to review and submit resumes from the convenience of your cell phone, and CareerBuilder has an iPhone application. Just about everything will be electronic in the future, so the need to brand yourself online will only grow.

Recruiters and hiring managers will use their cell phones to do background checks on candidates before, after, and even during interviews. Furthermore, live-casting and life-streaming video websites are starting to become mainstream. Yes, even Hollywood producers like Steven Spielberg have broadcasted online. What started out as *Justin.tv*, which entitles anyone to broadcast their life, has given rise to other services, such as UStream, Seesmic, Qik, Utterz, and Kyte.

> ### Mobile Social Networking
>
> By 2012, 18 percent of people will be engaged in social networks on mobile devices (eMarketer, 2008)[62].

You can be in a car, on a plane, or in an exotic location and find just about anyone who has a Facebook, LinkedIn, MySpace, Twitter, or blog profile. All media is going portable quickly, which should be a quick alert for you. With camera phones, digital cameras, and Web cameras, your brand can easily be exposed. Videos or pictures can be taken, uploaded to a video-sharing site, and then travel from blog to blog. After submission, your content can be read on the Kindle or seen on a phone. When you're online, you can be searchable through Google; when mobile devices have browser capabilities, your brand can be found just about anywhere, by anyone, at any time. Keep this in mind when developing your online brand.

Offline Brand Presence

No matter how many videos you distribute, how many blog posts your write, and how extraordinary your personal branding kit is, the real test is how you perform in reality. It's quite easy to represent— or misrepresent—yourself online, but in person, you simply can't get away with it. To have a powerful presence offline, you'll need to live and breathe every item in your personal branding tool kit.

There are countless places to network online, but there are lots of venues you can network offline, too, promoting your brand. My advice is to research your options and choose carefully. Participate in events that are most in sync with your brand, including special interest groups, industry summits and conventions, career fairs, and professional meet-ups.

Find out what opportunities exist in your area and attend events in your niche. Use each opportunity to network and learn about your chosen field. If possible, seek active membership in professional organizations that will help you achieve your goals. These look great on your resume, website, or blog!

Many professional organizations have special volunteer positions. These positions often come with various responsibilities, such as meeting organization, sponsorship management, or administrative duties. As a volunteer, you will have the opportunity to network and gain visibility with key people—which can really help you achieve your goals.

Use the interpersonal skills in your personal branding toolkit to network effectively offline. Treat each interaction as a new and important opportunity to promote your brand. Also, consider ordering customized business cards as a way to make a lasting brand impression.

The following tips will help you network effectively during offline events, but keep in mind that you can employ many of them online as well:

- **Establish goals.** Think of what you want to walk away with prior to participating so that you can better scope the situation, the type of people you're interested in meeting, and the end result. Maybe you're seeking new contacts or a few new facts that could stimulate business ideas.

- **Build trust.** Stay authentic and offer to be a resource to others to help sell yourself. Put yourself in their shoes; would you really want a conversation to be one-sided and purchase a product from someone you don't know yet? Product-purchasing behavior is driven by trust; the same goes for people.

- **Prepare and practice.** Know your personal brand statement cold so that when you start a conversation, you have a foundation to speak from. Your introduction should be clear, compelling, and delivered so that it resonates with your audience.

- **Scan the room and pick your points of contact.** People are at different points in their careers; some are represented by higher-quality brand names and have stronger networks than others. You should identify and associate with those who exemplify strong personal brands.

- **Names, names, and more names.** You will encounter many personal brands during these events, and remembering them will be quite challenging. Those who do remember names will have a competitive advantage, as people enjoy hearing their names and feeling like you care.

- **Use the event topic as a conversational piece.** After leading with your brand statement, you can easily bring in the topics covered in the event. If you're creative, you can share the experiences you've had that relate to that topic and ask questions.

- **Employ the two-step follow-up.** First, pass a business card to the person you're speaking with when he hints that he wants to move on or you feel the conversation is concluding. Second, just like after an interview, send this individual a follow-up email, letting him know that you will be a resource for him—and direct him to your blog or website if you have one (and you surely do, right?).

- **Be mindful of your appearance.** Your appearance not only involves dressing the part but also your body language. Project professionalism and confidence.

I joined the American Marketing Association in 2007 with the intention of developing my offline brand presence, learning more about marketing, discovering trends, and helping me to network as a youthful marketer. I soon realized that aside from consuming resources, such as webcasts and articles, at *marketingpower.com*, I was disconnected from the community. To solve this problem, I emailed the vice president of recruitment for the Boston chapter, explaining my credentials as well as how I wanted to be involved.

As a result, I was able to volunteer as the brand manager for the chapter. When I went to subsequent events, I got to know other volunteers. All the other volunteers wanted to be introduced to me, and through them, I was able to meet others. I kept in touch with volunteers both online and offline, and they have been following my career with personal branding ever since. I was even asked to be a keynote speaker, proving that I had climbed the networking hierarchy and reached the top. By being aggressive in this manner, I set myself up for networking success.

Consistent Online/Offline Branding

Your online and offline brand presence must be consistent. When corporate brands advertise products, they always issue one consistent message. You can benefit from the same strategy. Create a consistent message for your brand and apply it to all of your social networks, your blog, your business card, and even your resume.

Don't create a false expectation for those who get to know your eBrand who'll be disappointed when they meet you offline. Think about it: if you're on an online dating website and edit your picture to make yourself look like Brad Pitt or Nicole Kidman, your false representation will be a turnoff to the interested party when you actually meet. You need to focus on being yourself and letting people know your brand is one on which they can rely.

Having a consistent—and incredible—personal brand requires hard work and dedication. But if you're dedicated and create an online and offline brand presence that relates to the demands of your target audience and delivers what they're looking for, they will embrace it. When this happens, you'll be amazed to see how many opportunities for success open up to you!

Chapter 7

Step 3–Communicate Your Brand

There are billions of people in the world, but only a select few are celebrities. The world is full of individuals who could have made a difference but were never ambitious or prepared enough to show the world what they're capable of. Do you want to be a random face in an unknown crowd, or do you want to be one of the lucky few? If you want to make a positive impact and find success, now is the time to show and tell the world about brand *You*. To do so, communicating your brand is key.

Personal PR

Public relations is a great corporate or personal communication tool with the sole objective of advancing a brand image with the public and shielding it from damage. In recent years, traditional PR options have expanded, and the field has exploded with many new outlets. Once restricted to using journalists, reporters, and analysts as channels, PR now encompasses the blogosphere and the whole range of online media.

> " Social media has empowered people to become the new influencers, and it is forcing PR to recognize and include them in their communications strategies. "

—Brian Solis, president and founder, Future Works

There has been a transition from spending PR and advertising funds on traditional forms of media to investing in online options. According to Nielsen Online, there were over 330 million active Internet home users in 2008[63], and 28.2 percent of advertising will be spent online, compared to 21 percent percent spent on radio (eMarketer, 2007)[64]. In addition, print media will continue to lose its share of ad revenue as the online share grows (*New York Times*, 2007)[65]. And by 2011, over 86.6 percent of all Internet users will be loyal online video viewers (eMarketer, 2007)[66].

> " When you create your own brand online with a blog, video, or text, you suddenly have visibility with the world's most powerful people if the timing and topic are right. "

David Kirkpatrick, senior editor, *Fortune*

So what does this all mean for your brand? It's simple: as more people tune into media online, you have more of an opportunity to broadcast your brand and command exposure for your personal niche. That is not to say that if you appear on TV, the radio, or in print magazines, your brand won't gain exposure, but these expensive options are out of reach for most personal brands.

The Internet, by far the cheapest medium you can use to build an audience, is leveling the playing field.

From Online to Primetime

Here are some examples of people who have used their online reputation to achieve success in television:

- **Michael Buckley** hosts *What the Buck*, the most popular entertainment show on YouTube. With over 270,000 subscribers and spots mocking Britney Spears and other celebrities, Michael's brand has been elevated to Fox News, where he commentates on the *Lips & Ears* show[67].

- **Perez Hilton** has a celebrity gossip blog that is visited by millions, with hundreds of comments on each post. His popularity has given rise to a VH1 TV show entitled *What Perez Sez* (*New York Times*, 2007)[68].

Communicating your brand will get you discovered, and the Internet is a great tool for doing so. That's right: if you have a blog, you are seen as a "media practitioner." As your blog subscription base increases, advertisers are more likely to place ads on your website, and the probability that traditional media forms will write about it increases. Some of the most influential and prolific bloggers receive hundreds of project pitches each day.

Passive and Proactive Approaches

As you put on your personal PR hat, realize that you must now concern yourself with appealing to both mainstream and online media. There are both passive and proactive approaches to making this happen.

As your online presence grows, the press can passively discover you from a Google search on a topic that is reflected in a story they are currently writing. Also, through word-of-mouth or previous press, your name may be mentioned to journalists as a source. In 2008, Brodeur conducted a study on how influential blogs are to journalists' jobs. The results show that they really care about blogs. About 78 percent of journalists scour blogs in search of story ideas and new angles. Nearly 70 percent of all reporters check a blog list on a regular basis.

Then there are more proactive approaches, where you pitch stories to reporters who traditionally write about your niche. To locate them, you can go to their websites, review articles, and jot down contact information. PR Leads (*prleads.com*) is a subscription website that you can use, for $99 a month, to have queries from reporters looking for sources emailed directly to you each day. You can also sign up for the "If I Can Help a Reporter Out…" mailing list (*helpareporter.com*) and receive free queries from reporters.

If you really want high visibility, you can enlist the expertise of a PR agency. PR agencies already have the relationships and in-house expertise needed to get your name out, as long as you supply them with materials, but using an agency will cost much more than $99 a month. In addition, outsourcing and investing more time in building your brand comes at the cost of not forging relationships that can help you in the future for minimal cost.

The Personal Press Release

In 2007, I coined the term *personal press release*. Its meaning and purpose were clear: to announce one's brand to the world. My objective was to communicate my brand to others, but to do this, I had to wrap all of my work and achievements into a coherent and appealing story. My first release was centered on *DanSchawbel.com* and how it was the future of recruitment and self-promotion.

The release consisted of a clever pitch, full news summary, and multimedia components—including screen shots and images from my websites and links to corresponding articles. I also provided multiple contact points and sharing utilities so that the reader could easily contact me and (hopefully) spread the release to others.

Your Personal Press Release

Your personal press release should contain the following:

- **Headline.** A short and attention-grabbing title

- **News summary.** A short paragraph that reviews your personal story, including major milestones and distinctions

- **Personal summary.** A three-paragraph rendition of your personal story and accomplishments, using bullets for highlighted items

- **Relevant links.** Links to resources that highlight your brand, including your website, blog, and other sites to which you've contributed

- **Multimedia features.** Embedded video from YouTube or Viddler that promotes your brand

- **Sharing features.** Sharing services, such as Digg and Stumble-Upon, which are integrated into your press release if it's on a website, drawing more eyes to your release and giving it longevity

---

With limited PR proficiency as a 24-year-old, I made the common mistake of blasting out an extensive pitch while attaching the PDF file to each email I sent to newspapers, magazines, and even a few bloggers. I was looking to distribute my brand through any means possible, but since I was an unknown, my message wasn't always relevant or eagerly received. Luckily for me, there were no repercussions, as many bloggers have posted inappropriate pitches on their blogs. I did, however, teach myself not to blanket-pitch to media and to set realistic goals. Consider my experience before you pitch your brand to the media.

The Personal Press Kit

Aside from a personal press release, you may choose to build a compilation of your brand in the form of a press kit. You don't have to be famous or an expert in your field to have your own press kit. I believe anyone can—and should—create a press kit that serves as a differentiating tool and a clever way of displaying your many talents. As you move forward in your career, your kit can evolve alongside your new accomplishments.

The purpose of a press kit is to give the media, your clients, and recruiters a full sense of who you are and what you can provide. It is also a great way to catalog all your achievements. You cannot substitute a resume for this kit—it's targeted toward the media, whereas a resume is intended for hiring managers.

There are eight sections in your *personal press kit*, which should be in a PDF format. You can convert a Word document to PDF by using the "Save As" command. If you need help, go to *doc2pdf.net* to convert your document.

1: **Cover page.** The first page of the kit must capture the reader's attention and convey meaning. Include your name, brand statement, headshot picture, and any other relevant design elements you feel would be appealing. Remember to title it "Press Kit."

2: **Bio.** For this section, write a two-paragraph summary, concentrating on the major milestones in your career or education. You can summarize your resume if that helps. Next to your bio, consider including another picture of yourself to reinforce your image in the minds of your readers.

3: **Testimonials.** Gather endorsements from reputable supervisors, coworkers, professors, or clients. The more prestigious the person is, the better you will look. Be sure to ask permission to use these endorsements—for your press kit, on your references list, and for mentioning when you interview for jobs.

4: Experience. A press kit isn't a resume, so don't include three bullets next to each job you've had. Instead, list the major projects you've worked on and the results you've delivered, both quantitatively and qualitatively.

5: Associations. List all relevant memberships in associations, organizations, societies, and clubs in your kit. You never know when you can make a connection with someone reading your kit who happens to be a member of one of those groups.

6: Media/publications. If you've written or been written about or quoted or have established your own media outlet, that information should appear in your press kit. In my press kit, I note my blog, TV show, magazine, and awards—with screen shots and descriptions of each.

7: Public speaking. A lot of people who have press kits use them to solicit speaking inquiries. In this section, you can list the audiences you've spoken to, the types of talks or workshops you can give, and details regarding what they should expect from your performance. You can also include a testimonial or pictures from a previous event.

8: Contact info. Since a press kit can be printed out and distributed separately from your other marketing materials, you need to list your contact information. This could be your phone or fax number, email, website, blog, instant messaging screen name, Skype name, etc.

The Art of Email

Most communication these days exists through email, which is why it's especially important to communicate your personal brand within your messages. For all of you who use screen names that contain no trace of your actual name, you need to alter your behavior if you want others to associate your email address with your brand name (this means you, "GoOfBaall382" and "beachgal09").

When emailing your resume, cover letter, references document, or even touching base with a friend or contact, you should use an email name and signature that reflect your brand. For example, I use *dan.schawbel@gmail.com* so the receiver knows exactly who is sending the message.

A lot of businesspeople question whether to use their business email or personal email when communicating. The answer to that is to apply your personal email address if you are an entrepreneur or sole proprietor or when corresponding with a friend. If you are a part of a corporation, then use your business email while at work and personal outside of work. Again, your email signature could contain your blog address, feed, homepage URL, phone number, email address, and personal brand statement. This is your decision to make, based on the goals of your brand. With some creativity, you can make your emails stand out.

The New Rules of Engagement

When you step forth into the Web 2.0 world, you will notice that "giving before receiving" is a common courtesy and part of the culture. My favorite magazine is *Fast Company*, and by scanning *fastcompany.com*, I came across a columnist who writes about my topic. I left her a personal note through her email, and our relationship began. I wrote a blog post highlighting her achievements as a public relations expert—without being provoked in any way. By giving before receiving, I was able to build a strong relationship with her, increasing the likelihood that she would write about me.

When I was growing up, I noticed that people who asked me to do things for them were labeled "users." My parents had always said to stay away from these types of people because they weren't true friends. The words "I want" became so obnoxious, repetitive, and selfish that I started ignoring them altogether. My feelings were shared by many of my loyal friends, who would complain about these types of people.

I'd gotten to this approach to relationships, until I entered the blogosphere and received emails from people who actually wanted to help me out, without asking for anything in return. I was shocked by these gestures and was really excited that the world had become a friendlier place—until I realized that giving was a great strategy for getting things in return. Use the Internet culture to your brand's advantage. The following sample message can serve as a guide for constructing your own strategic emails.

From: Dan Schawbel

To: Mr. Matthews

Subject: News Story—Conquering the Recruitment Process Using Social Media

Dear Mr. Matthews,

I just read your article in the *Wall Street Journal* about personal empowerment in the workplace. I not only agree with your findings and analysis but have discovered that social media can build confidence and personal branding can bridge people with opportunities.

Recently, I was able to reverse the roles of recruitment and was hired internally as a firm's first social media specialist based on my external work. By leveraging the reach of social networks and blogs, individuals can be empowered, network, and display their talents in a way never before possible. Below is my success story as I confronted and commanded the recruitment process, after being a victim during college.

More information can be found here:
www.PressReleaseHomepage.com.

Best wishes,

Dan Schawbel

Follow the rules of successful personal and professional letter writing when constructing emails. If the intent of your message is to impress the reader, do you think sloppy spelling and grammar, or slang, will do the trick? Take your emails seriously; your online presence will be heavily shaped by how your emails are perceived. These days, your shot at making a first impression might occur over email. Don't you want it to be a positive one?

Maintain Good Blogger Relations

These days, many people trust certain bloggers more than traditional journalists, because blogs act as objective consumer reports. But before soliciting prominent and influential bloggers, be aware that they can extract any part of your message and blog about it. Therefore, they have the freedom and privilege of either making or breaking your reputation. Proceed with caution!

The following are some rules for maintaining good *blogger relations*:

- **Be active.** Don't just pitch to the blogger; become an active participant by commenting on the blog. Bloggers get pitched all the time, so differentiating your approach is critical.

- **Listen and learn.** Before initiating an email, comment, or phone dialog with the target blogger, review at least five of their most recent posts and/or podcasts. This will allow you to get a better sense of their writing style, as well as their brand. A blog centered on emerging technology will probably not take pitches from an individual who just opened her own fast-food franchise.

- **Links are currency.** By linking from your blog to their blog (*trackback*), you are catching their attention and increasing their authority level on Technorati. This "link love" is benefiting the blogger's cause—and the probability that they will aid your cause increases.

- **Strategize and execute.** Don't blindly pitch to 200 bloggers. Instead, focus your attempts on the most popular and influential bloggers in your niche. Note that influential bloggers with vast readership will spread your brand across other blogs through trackbacks. Don't be surprised if traditional journalists, who subscribe to these influential blogs, write about you as well.

- **Don't be their spam.** Personalize each communication so that you connect with your target audience. This is especially important for the subject line of your email, which needs to stand out among all the other emails a popular blogger gets daily.

- **Keep it simple and concise.** Anyone involved in media has very little patience and time for viewing pages of information unless it's explicitly tied to a story they are currently working on. Write a few short sentences and some bullet points to highlight your major points before sending your email.

- **Be open—but closed.** Honesty, integrity, and openness is always appreciated by bloggers. But if you reveal too much information, especially if it's personal, they have the power to blog about it right then and there. Watch what you say, because it can be used against you.

- **Be enticing.** If you can provide free resources and customize your message to reflect the blogger's current writing and interest areas, you will be more successful.

The key to successful public relations is to create relationships. Would you rather send a Hail Mary email to someone you've never met before and possibly be the victim of bad publicity online or send a quick email to a friend asking for help? The answer is obvious, so focus on the relationship first and your self-promotion second. Effective PR can produce visibility and perceived value for your personal brand.

Other Strategies for Announcing Your Brand

Aside from communicating with the media and maintaining relationships, there are a few other strategies you can implement—starting today. Every time you think about where you are going to promote your brand, consider your target audience: Is it the audience you want to reach? Next, research and discover sources that already market to your audience. By contributing to a variety of media outlets, assembling a team of *evangelists*, and attending and creating events for self-promotion, your brand will take off like a rocket!

Contribute to Various Media Outlets

While forging a community around my blog, commenting on other blogs, and directing a series of podcasts, I wrote articles for a variety of media, including magazines and online sites. Contributing to various media sources is one of the best ways to position your brand. Why is this so crucial? Your blog may have a confined readership base, but other media might have already accumulated lots of subscribers. Don't forget: it's easier to reach an audience that already exists than to find a new audience. It works the same with current and prospective customers—keeping current customers satisfied is much easier than attracting new business.

Consider the following content contribution guidelines as you get started:

- **Start small.** Approach small websites first before going after larger media conglomerates. Start small and continuously build a freelance portfolio, evidence that you've already been published. Then give the big guns a shot.
- **Word count.** Articles don't have to be lengthy and can range from 200 to 2,500 words. The more expertise and confidence you have on a topic, the less time and fewer words you will need to complete an article.

- **Use quotes.** If you base your article around a story, with examples and quotes from credible brands, you will have more luck getting published.

- **Submit to article directories.** Become an author on Ezine @rticles (*ezinearticles.com*), which is a collection of hundreds of expert articles in a single repository. Over 100,000 writers submit their work, and you can be one of them!

Brand Evangelism

My *Personal Branding Magazine* gathered a flock of evangelists who operate as both contributors and promoters. Evangelists are walking advertisements who voice their opinion on a corporation, product, or person, creating a buzz factor. They not only share their valuable knowledge by writing articles, but they let others know the magazine exists through their websites. As previously stated, people are more inclined to support your project if their brand is part of it. It's hard to make your personal brand go viral without dedicated evangelists.

Locating evangelists doesn't require a navigation system. Think of your blog as a magnet that attracts people who want to be part of the bigger picture. People who aren't interested in your brand won't comment on your posts, link to your blog, or subscribe. Your blog and networks are magnets, repelling noninterested parties and attracting others.

Chances are, you already have evangelists; you just don't recognize them. Your family and friends have the deepest relationship with you and know what you're capable of, so it is far easier for them to communicate your brand message. You should never underestimate the power of your existing network.

Start Your Own Event

Events don't just happen; people make them happen. As the commander of your career, you can gather your contacts together, ask them to invite their network, and then stage an event where you can showcase your expertise on a topic, your creative expertise, or your useful products. Having an event series is a great way to keep in touch with people and brand yourself in the process.

> **Despite social networking, in-person networking is the ultimate form of brand building if you're networking with the right people.**
>
> —David Kirkpatrick, senior editor, *Fortune*

Have you ever gone to a house party or club and sought out the host or hostess? If you have, then you know that by positioning yourself as an event leader, you will gain attention, recognition, and status. Maybe you've gone to a successful networking event, convention, or fair and wished they occurred more often. If you host them, they can happen whenever you want!

Use the following tips to help you host your own event:

- **Make it worthwhile.** To set up an event, you need a theme and a plan for getting people to attend. People don't go out of their way to attend events unless they feel that they will gain knowledge, network with others, receive an incentive, or have fun.

- **Find influential attendees.** Lure the right people to your event by getting the right influencers and role models agree to attend. If your resources are limited, then get creative—think of ways to convince these influential people why they'll benefit from coming to your event.

- **Promote through social media.** Blogs allow you to reach your community directly, promote your event, and follow up after the event to receive feedback. Wikis have been employed as guest lists too—as each individual signs up for your event, she can add her name and address to the webpage. Twitter can be used to notify others when and where your event is located. Again, do your best to make your event seem worth your audience's time.

- **Good timing counts.** Scheduling the event around breakfast, lunch, or dinner is a good idea because it's in everyone's routine anyway. Stay away from holidays and odd hours. Consider surveying a few key members of your audience to see when their schedules are open.

- **Have food and activities.** Having food and drink and engaging activities at your event is a great way to get people interested in attending and keep them from falling asleep.

- **Guest speakers.** If you know any humorous, resourceful, or reputable guest speakers, they will not only help build the credibility of your event but gain exposure to your audience as well.

- **Gather cohosts.** The more people you have helping to organize your event, the better.

Make sure to make the most of your event; if it's a successful one, then you can use that great momentum to attract more people to future events. Consider using social media before and after the event to further promote your brand. The following suggestions will help you get started:

- **Upcoming.org.** This social network lists corporate events, conferences, and special interest groups. After you sign up, you can add events that you will be attending or start your own. It's a great way to let people know what you're doing and promote the event.

- **Flickr.** Try to find someone to take pictures at your event. If you find someone at the event taking pictures, connect with them after the event so you can repurpose the pictures to promote brand *You.*

- **YouTube.** Try to have your event videotaped. After the event, edit it down to the best ten minutes and post it to YouTube.

- **Slideshare.net.** Care to share Microsoft PowerPoint slides from your event with attendees? This website will convert your deck into a virtual online presentation, which can be shared and commented on by users.

- **Blogs.** To demonstrate what your typical events are like, showcase past events on your blog or website. You can even embed your presentation from *SlideShare*, a video of your presentation from YouTube, and event photos from Flickr.

The bottom line is that if your resources are limited, it falls upon your shoulders to communicate your brand. There are lots of resources available for you to be your own personal PR professional. So get motivated, develop a plan of attack, and make it happen. You—and your brand—are worth the effort!

Chapter 8

Step 4—Maintain Your Brand

Never forget: your brand is a representation of who you are—it's brand YOU! As you progress through your life, you'll grow, mature, and develop—and so will your brand. At some point, you may even redefine your brand, based on new passions and discoveries. Just as major corporations have modified their brand messaging over time to match their audience and current trends, individuals should update and maintain their personal brands on a regular basis.

Maintaining your brand entails performing routine maintenance, or "spring cleaning." You never want someone to venture to your website and review outdated materials or hear someone call you unimaginative or out of date. As you update your brand, be mindful that your reputation is on the line and that it's very easy to lose face and be a victim of a lost opportunity.

Reputation Management

In today's competitive career marketplace, you need to stay relevant to survive. One way to achieve relevancy is constantly to acquire new skills. Ideally, you should work toward acquiring all the different skills and techniques that match the requirements of new positions that may unfold along your career path. This way, you can sustain a competitive advantage and communicate a strong message of relevancy and effectiveness to your audience. Incorporate these skills in your personal branding kit in order to improve your current organizational role or change career paths.

Your Brand Is Searchable

While taking a shower or sleeping in bed, do you know who is searching for your personal eBrand? Wonder if you've ever been Googled before going on a date? These days, with the rise of social networking sites, blogs, forums, and search engines like Google, anything is possible. Journalists may be searching for sources for their next big article. Employers and friends might Google your name to verify your identity and background. There are even people-specific search engines that target individuals while hiding corporate results (*123people.com, spock.com, zoominfo.com*).

> Believe in and search for a reflection of your brand's reach and reputation. Either you work to actively maintain it, or someone or something else appears at the top of the search results.
>
> —Aaron Wall, search engine optimization (SEO) expert and author of SEOBook.com

Why should you stay aware of search results on your name? At any point in time, you could be subject to a personal brand disaster, where your name gets a negative connotation. The viral capabilities of the Internet means that information, opinions, and flat-out libel can spread pretty fast; careful maintenance of your brand is the best way to keep control over what is said and shown about you online.

Use the following tips to maintain your brand's reputation online:

- **Google your name periodically.** View the results and see if they best represent your brand.

- **Set a Google alert for your name.** Each day, you will receive a notification citing your name in any articles that were written. Search for your name on *blogsearch.google.com* (blogs written about you) and then click a subscription option, such as RSS or email. You can also do the same with *news.google.com* to search for your appearance on traditional news sites.

- **Concentrate on a few social networks.** These might include *Facebook*, LinkedIn, and your blog. These tend to have the most users, so they are more worth your time and effort than more obscure venues. If you go to google.com/alerts and set "comprehensive" alert for your name it will take care of blogs, news, and more.

- **Keep in touch with your evangelists.** They can keep a close eye out for you and report back if they notice any unusual activity. You don't have to ask them to complete this chore; your true evangelists will record results for you on their own.

- **Use Technorati.** Use this site as both a people-search engine and to check trackbacks to see who is using the information on your blog for their own. Search for your name on Technorati and then subscribe to the results, as you would for a Google alert.

- **Monitor discussion boards.** You can use BoardTracker Discussion Search (*boardtracker.com*) to search through any threads that contain your name.

- **Monitor Twitter.** Typing in your name at *search.twitter.com* will allow you to find any messages that cite your name. This is especially important because

Twitter messages travel very fast and you can keep an eye out for anyone who mentions you.

- **Monitor blog comments.** The website *backtype.com* will trace every blog where you comment or where someone comments about you. This service allows you to find, follow, and share comments across the Web.

The Google Effect

In this electronic age, you must monitor and influence your brand's activity on popular search engines like Google. It's important to note that as you build your brand reputation, you must invest significant time in ensuring integrity and accuracy. For example, if you write a controversial blog post, you may attract the wrong attention and offend either your community or someone who is browsing. She can then blog about it and, when a hiring manager Googles your name, you will lose a valuable opportunity. One incident can have a lasting effect on your brand. You never want to Google your name and find that you are misrepresented by a blogger. Set a weekly or daily schedule to oversee all activity concerning your brand online.

> ### Google Woes
>
> Famous celebrities have had their own Google woes. Here are some celebrities that I Googled in early 2008:
>
> - **Wesley Snipes.** When Googling his name, his conviction for tax avoidance showed up in four out of the top ten results.
>
> - **Vivica Fox.** She had the same number of results as Wesley but for her alleged sex tape video; the results also included a YouTube video of her interview on the topic.

- **Ray Liotta.** I discovered a very interesting website called "Ray Liotta makes me want to kill myself."

- **Amy Winehouse.** Like Ray, she has a special website dedicated to her entitled "When will Amy Winchouse die—Predict it here!"

- **Isaiah Thomas.** His Wikipedia entry notes his racism and sexual harassment lawsuit. I also observed more entries in Google for this lawsuit, drawing even more attention to the negative aspect of his brand.

You need to focus on blogging and maintaining your personal website to ensure your name has an impact in Google. Remember, Google keeps records of every comment, blog post, *bylined article*, and video you produce, and if your name isn't traceable in Google, then to the online world, you don't exist. In this way, Google searchability is a measure of your personal brand's strength. The more results for your name that appear in a Google search, the more influential your brand will be.

With common names like Smith and Clark, it's nearly impossible to be found in Google. Years ago, people thought that sharing a name with a celebrity was special, but now it counts against them. When you Google Britney Spears, you will receive millions of results, but if you share that name, you will be buried on the 60 millionth page. If your name matches a celebrity's, you need to focus on differentiating yourself by middle name or with a quick catch phrase. When you have a unique name, it's far easier to stand out and control your rankings. I'm not recommending you change your name but rather that you think of creative strategies to bring your name to life. If your name is distinct, give your parents a hug.

> ❝ We face a challenge our parents never had to deal with. Not only do I need to have an impeccable resume and job experience by the time I graduate, but I also need to manage my Web identity to make sure that my potential employers get the proper impression when they Google me. ❞
>
> —Jennifer Vargas, graduating senior, Cornell University

I've heard stories in which *YourName.com* domain names are purchased as holiday or birthday presents to secure a child's future. There are even baby-naming consultants who help parents contrive names that aren't popular in Google. In a world regulated by Google, your brand must be found and managed simultaneously. We must always monitor our status on the Web.

Online Damage Control

When you notice a website or blog that exposes you negatively, you need to have a disaster recovery strategy, just as corporations do. There are several courses of action you can initiate in response to bad publicity.

- You can comment on the other blog, revealing the truth to that blogger's community.
- You can post your side of the story on your blog or website.
- You can ignore it and do absolutely nothing.
- You can contact the blogger or website owner directly, politely explain why his information is false—or apologize—and hope the blogger edits his post or posts a follow-up.

To prevent disasters, try your hardest to stay true to your brand—if you stray from who you are, you may become the target of bad publicity. In addition, with digital cameras and voice recorders so readily available, it's easy for someone to blackmail you by posting an embarrassing video or audio file on the Web, where it can be shared by millions. You can be the object of these attacks online or offline. Anything you say or do can be used against you in a Web 2.0 world.

Fight Back with Search Engine Optimization (SEO)

Google controls your online reputation, but it wasn't created to serve that purpose. It is a central hub for information that ranks sites according to importance, using an algorithm. As the leading search engine, Google uses Web crawlers to review sites at a rapid pace and deliver relevant results to the user. You have the power to influence Google's results and establish a noticeable presence in the first few pages for your name.

> With the right knowledge and resources, you can impact the results search engines show for specific queries, pushing down negative listings and replacing them with positive ones.
>
> —Rand Fishkin, CEO and founder, SEOmoz.org

Use the following tips for maximizing your search engine results:

- **Domain and title.** Your name or company name should be included in both your domain name and homepage title. For instance, I combined my *DanSchawbel.com* domain purchase with a matching "Dan Schawbel" title. If you want to associate your name with the business you're running or a special topic, change your site's title to "Dan Schawbel: Personal Branding Expert" so viewers to make the connection between you and that subject area.
- **Key Words.** Search engine users type in a series of one or more key words in hopes they will find websites that

match their interests. Behind the scenes, Web crawlers analyze websites for key words and provide users with the top results that match their queries. What does this mean for you? After selecting the right key words, the following are best practices for including them on your Web page:

Density: The percentage of key words relative to the total number of words on a given page. You should aim for a ratio of 3–6 percent. To analyze your page for key word density, go to *live-keyword-analysis.com*.

Frequency: The number of times a key word appears in a Web page. The more times you use a key word, the more relevant your page becomes in terms of a Google search for that word. Instead of trying to cheat the system by using a key word 100 times, use your best judgment. About 12–17 key words for a 400-word page is acceptable and encouraged. After all, you want your writing to be coherent!

Proximity: This refers to how close together the key words are. The general rule is to place key words close together to form groups of key words. For instance, you would want to keep "search engine optimization" together instead of separate, because people search for that phrase.

Prominence: Search engines prefer you to use key words near the top of your Web page in locations such as in the title and heading tags.

- **Meta tags.** When you develop your website, you need to use meta tags to describe what people will get when they view your site. There are three main tags you need to worry about: title, description, and key words. These tags go in the HTML markup page of your website. To have these tags automatically generated for you, go to *addme.com/meta.htm*.

- **Page freshness.** Standard websites are updated infrequently. Typically, they are revised and lengthened when new product features come out or when individuals modify their work experience to reflect their current situation. Blogs are intuitive tools that allow you to populate a new page for each post you write. Each blog post is indexed by search engines, and your page's "newness" drives PageRank. Pages that were written in 1999 are less pertinent than those in 2008 and so on. On the other hand, the historical presence of your site lends it overall credibility and is, therefore, appreciated by search engines.

- **Site traffic.** The number of website visitors you have tells Google that your site is a popular source of information. Although SEO may help your traffic skyrocket, there are other ways of driving visitors to your site, such as guest-posting on blogs and social networks.

- **Page contents.** The content on your page should be consistent and on-topic. Page titles are seen first by search engines, so include desired key words in them. For example, if your site is about your bakery, be sure to include key words such as *cake* and *croissant*. Content is extremely important to becoming a hot destination. People generally link to content that is compelling, controversial, or insightful.

- **Links system.** Links are the holy grail of SEO. Your PageRank will increase as more sites link to yours. A PageRank of 5 or more usually has thousands of backlinks. Each link is a vote from that website approving yours. The sites with the greatest PageRanks will substantially increase your own if you receive a link from them.

  External linking: Performing link exchanges is the simplest transaction you can have with another website owner. You each add each other's link to a designated page, which increases PageRank™ equally. Start with websites that have similar content and status to yours and build up. Even if you don't exchange links, you can always link to a source with more background information on your topic. Sometimes you may even be surprised by a reciprocal link by that website in the future.

Internal linking. You also want to have an internal system, where you link back and forth through various pages within your site. For blogs, linking to an old post to reinforce your point or carry a conversation is a plus. The PageRank of one page can have an impact on another if you use this strategy.

Social networking and blogging are two of the latest and greatest trends for conquering Google. You will notice that some popular social networks carry a lot of weight in Google. Facebook, LinkedIn, Technorati, YouTube, and Twitter are all positive influences on your search rank because they contain millions of personal profiles, which each have unique addresses. They are all highly trafficked websites, contain personal information, and have a lot of link-backs that promote to your brand.

> **If you are trying to build a personal brand, one thing that is a must is to create a website and use search engine optimization so that you can rank for terms related to what you do, as well as your own name.**
>
> —Neil Patel, chief technical officer, ACS

You should join these popular services so that you can "own your brand" on Google. If you have negative publicity associated with your brand, by joining these networks, you can push those results down. Then if someone Googles you, your personal brand will be secure. Blogging is the easiest way to climb to the top, as blogs are updated more regularly and there are more link-backs within blogs that propel your rank.

An important thing to keep in mind is that SEO is always unstable terrain. Google changes its algorithm randomly, and you might get your desired results one day and not the next. Also, Google is not the sole distributor of your brand—pieces of your brand are stored within a variety of online websites. The bottom line is that participating in new media poses opportunities and challenges and requires constant attention and vigilance.

Privacy Is Golden

With the onslaught of social networks, we want some information revealed—and some concealed. Want an example? If you think that the information you contribute to the profiles on Facebook is private, think again. Personal information is all tangled in what is called a "social graph," which is a cyberdepiction of your real-life social network developed by Facebook. MySpace has even more problems with privacy, especially with the sheer number of fictitious "members" that are created as viruses. They add you, and if you accept, you spam all of your friends.

The new generation is more inclined to give up personal information just to join these networks. However, it's not just teenagers and students who participate anymore. More than 74 percent of adults routinely give out their information online, including their email address and birthday, according to the National Cyber Security Alliance (NCSA). People are willing to spread their information from network to network without fear, until their identity is stolen, they receive spam and other unwanted email, or they are the victim of cyberstalking or a computer virus.

A great way to protect your brand name is to determine which information should and should not be digitized. College students have been notorious for posting explicit pictures on social networking sites, such as in Facebook profiles. We must be aware that the Internet is a public domain, so we should withhold all information we'd prefer to keep private.

Social networking sites do give you some options. They provide a privacy area, where you can regulate what information you make readily available, as well as keep hidden. Take advantage of these options to protect you and your brand from the dangers lurking online.

Social Network Privacy Tips

- Set limited access to your profiles to keep certain people separated from your personal information.

- Block users who either solicit you for business or send explicit messages that could cause harm.

- Don't include any information you don't want the public to see, such as your cell phone number.

- Promote your profiles to your network and stay clear of strangers that are just using social networks to build lists for their businesses.

Preventing Online Identity Theft

In cyberspace, more information is being created about you than you create yourself (IDC). As you spread yourself through social networks, your personal information is made available to lurkers, hackers, and database marketers.

- **Lurkers** may be observing your information because they are a friend or acquaintance or are genuinely interested in your brand.

- **Database marketers** are retrieving your personal information, including your location, product preferences, and contact information, in an effort to sell you things and make a profit.

- **Hackers** are desperately trying to uncover your user information for nefarious reasons—to steal your money or as a form of evil entertainment and sport.

Your personal eBrand may also be subject to another threat—identity theft. When you open accounts with multiple social networks, have a Web-based email service and a blog, and sign up for online access to your bank accounts and PayPal, you become particularly vulnerable to this terrible threat. With so many online sources that store your personal information, you must be careful about what information you share and how you store it. Did you know that most people use the same user name and passwords for all their online experiences? Believe it or not, much of this information is freely available on the Web and only a Google search away.

> " Failure to be proactive in the management of your online identity could lead to others making unfair claims about you, competitors undermining your good name, or worse... "
>
> —Andy Beal, Internet marketing consultant and coauthor of *Radically Transparent*

I learned this the hard way when I registered for Gmail and PayPal—without maintaining different passwords for these essential accounts. I had no disaster recovery strategy to use if something were to go sour. Then it happened. Someone got my log-in information and abused it, and I lost full access to all of these accounts. I lost hundreds of emails on my Gmail account, including messages about business opportunities, key contact information, and important notes from friends. Also, by losing my Google account, I lost access to the Google Group I had first used to gather contributors for my magazine.

As for PayPal, I lost a lot of money, as well as my entire magazine subscription base—each of whom received an email saying their subscription had ended. My email address is not just how I communicate with others, it's also part of my brand identity. Just knowing that someone could use my email account to contact members of my network with slander and hurtful comments really affected me. Suddenly, someone else—a complete stranger—was in control of my life.

I had to act quickly before any more damage could be done. After several tough weeks, I was able to recuperate from the incident. I learned a great deal from the ordeal; it opened my eyes to the dangers that lurk online and convinced me to develop an ongoing maintenance routine to keep this from happening again. Use the following tips for protecting and recovering your personal brand identity.

Before identity theft occurs, do the following:

- **Enter all your contacts into a database.** Do this as you make new contacts for networking purposes and to be able to reconnect if you suffer a loss. You can use Microsoft Excel, Access, or another program to accomplish this. Export contacts from your LinkedIn database and store them as well.

- **Purchase external and online storage.** Having these backups will prevent anxiety, minimize financial damage, and provide you with multiple recovery points. The cost per gigabyte (GB) of space these days makes backup storage a worthwhile investment. You can get a terabyte (1,000 GB) for less than $300. Xdrive offers 5 GB of online storage space for free, and Mozy (home edition) provides automatic backup of your files during scheduled times. FYI: My computer died while I was writing this book, and this is how I recovered my files!

- **Use multiple, complex passwords.** Apply this strategy to all your online assets, including your email account, electronic bank account, and website hosting services. If you're having trouble remembering them, write them down in a secret space and refer to them often, so you eventually commit them to memory. Verify the strength of your passwords at *microsoft.com/protect/yourself/ password/checker.mspx.*

- **Secure your blog content.** Register at Creative Commons, a site that provides protections and freedoms for authors. Also, you can manage all your copyrights online to protect yourself from misuse across the Internet. Automatically back up your blog content at *blogbackuponline.com.*

- **Register your name at all the mainstream social networks.** Doing this will secure your presence and prevent people from taking over your identity. As your brand flourishes, your name will be sought out by people who are against what you stand for or are trying to make a quick buck. Don't allow others opportunities to use your good name. To check name availability on various social networks, go to *usernamecheck.com.*

To recover *after* identity theft, do the following:

- **Reach out to key members of your network.** They may have contact information for others in your network and can help you recover any lost contact information. One tactic I employed was to post on my blog about the incident and ask my community for help. Before long, loyal readers had sent me comforting emails and comments. It was also a good way to raise awareness regarding identity theft and share ways for how to recover.

- **Call and email the companies that handle your assets.** Be sure to make them aware of the situation and let them investigate; after all, it's their problem as well as yours.

- **Register for new accounts with your account providers.** Start recovering your information while they help you solve the issue. You should constantly follow up to see how their investigations are progressing.

- **Get your mind off of the problem.** Focus on regenerating your personal brand. You're doing all you can; now it's time to move on with your life.

As the volume of social networks and online services increases and the number of hackers and greedy opportunists eager to steal your personal information grows, it becomes increasingly important for you to protect yourself—and your brand—from all threats. Identity theft will continue to become more common, and as we continue to live more of our lives online, identity theft's potential harm will grow. Protecting brand YOU should be among your main priorities, so take it seriously and do everything in your power to prevent becoming a victim.

Part III:
Now You Have Command

Chapter 9

Your Entrepreneurial Conquest

Attention, entrepreneurs and future masters of the universe! Now that you have a strong sense of your personal brand's identity and goals, it's time to embark on your journey toward success.

A lot of people are afraid to escape their "secure" day job and take the sort of risks that starting your own business from scratch entails. Other people get bored easily, don't like the constrictions of working for someone else, and are hungry for much more than a full plate of routine work assigned to them by their bosses. Is this you? Take the quiz in Figure 9.1, which will help you determine if you might be an entrepreneur. Place a check next to each description that fits you.

	Figure 9.1. Am I an Entrepreneur?	
1.	I don't like conforming to the status quo.	☐
2.	I want control and power over my life.	☐
3.	I am on a constant search for new opportunities.	☐
4.	I like to create things.	☐
5.	I prefer not to be managed and enjoy being in control.	☐
6.	I hate not coming in first.	☐
7.	I have a strong personal vision for my career path.	☐
8.	I like the challenges of starting a new project.	☐
9.	I don't like taking no for an answer.	☐
10.	I am a forward thinker and look to the future.	☐

Does your quiz contain more checkmarks than blanks? If so, then you might be a natural entrepreneur! Entrepreneurs are leaders, self-starters, and risk takers who collect the most profit—but often assume great risk and responsibility. Any aspiring entrepreneur should be mindful about taking a leap from the day job. But if you're up for the challenge, then this chapter will help you determine how to take brand YOU out on its own—and be successful!

Brand Characteristics of an Entrepreneur

After meeting many entrepreneurs, I've come to realize that they all share similar characteristics. Some people are born with an entrepreneurial spirit, while others acquire it through life experience after discovering their passions and goals. The following attributes will help you understand what qualities can help you win the entrepreneurship game.

Vision

Entrepreneurs look to the future, not just the present, and learn from past successes and failures to help them make the right decisions going forward. They have a clear vision of what they want to achieve, not just in one year but 10 or 15 years ahead—as well as a good sense of the direction they'd like to take with their lives.

The entrepreneurial mind must have a destination and set of goals, so it can work every day to head toward that destination and achieve success. I didn't just create a blog, magazine, podcast, and book without having a larger vision that combines everything I've done. You need to think big! Start to pull your vision together once you have cemented your brand goals and have a clear sense of the direction you'd like to take your career. Don't be afraid to promote your vision to your network; remember, having the support of those who are in a position to lend help and guidance is invaluable.

Creativity

Entrepreneurs aren't looking to steal ideas or use what has already been done. They need to think creatively and formulate their own unique ideas and plans, based on what they enjoy and what the market needs. Creativity is also important when it comes to being a successful entrepreneur. Marketing a business either requires a budget or ideas for creative promotional strategies. This also applies to promoting yourself.

Unconventional Marketing Strategies

Here are some examples of some creative and unconventional marketing strategies:

- Swiss International Air Lines placed ads on cars that were covered with snow in summer.

- eBay Belgium cleverly placed "Moved to eBay" signs after a few neighborhood stores closed down.

- Sony France placed "Don't Walk Alone" bright light messages around creepy places in Paris.

- *FHM* magazine projected a 60-foot-high image of Gail Porter's backside onto the Houses of Parliament to promote its 1999 poll to find the world's sexiest women.

Although these are established brands, they invested much more in creative thinking than in huge advertising budgets.

Tenacity

If you are a laid-back person, then you might not want to be an entrepreneur. Entrepreneurs are go-getters. They will do whatever it takes to conquer all obstacles and climb all mountains to succeed. They get very little sleep because they realize the opportunity cost in sleeping instead of getting things done. Personally, I won't even go to bed until I connect with close business associates in my network. Entrepreneurs have to make decisions and stick with them. There are no gray areas—no room for uncertainty!

Passion

You need to be so enthusiastic about your product or service that your face lights up like a Christmas tree every time you talk about it to people. If your idea doesn't excite you enough that it affects your emotions and body language, then maybe you need to choose something else. Entrepreneurs are so passionate about their businesses, they can actually instill good feelings in other people and get them excited about their businesses, which is an essential skill to attract investors, employees, or customers. When I talk about personal branding, I'm certainly not shy and laid-back—I'm determined to convince the world of its importance!

Problem-Solving Skills

Entrepreneurs think quickly on their feet. If an issue arrives, such as a customer service problem, then they must be able to solve the problem immediately—or delegate the responsibility for doing so to the right person. Also, your business should be customer focused, meaning that everything you do should benefit the end user, benefiting you in the long run. By taking problems seriously, particularly those of your customer and client base, your business gains credibility and customer loyalty and becomes increasingly in demand. Take problems seriously and work toward finding the best solutions, usually the ones with the lowest cost and highest impact.

Highly Competitive

Do you like tie games in sports? If so, then you may not have the competitive drive that often makes a successful entrepreneur. Entrepreneurs are extremely competitive individuals who are constantly strengthening their brands, products, and services to far exceed the competition. This attribute makes businesses better, which means consumers get more value for their dollar. Entrepreneurs don't know the meaning of losing or going out of business. They constantly research competitors and market against them. Are you dedicated to making your brand shine no matter what? If so, then go make it happen!

Emerging Entrepreneurs—You Are the Company!

When you start your journey as an entrepreneur, you will wear many different hats. You will be the CEO, CPO, CIO, CFO, and, of course, CMO of your personal brand! Even if you build an entire organization, you will still have to be knowledgeable in these areas to manage the people who do them, stay on top of things, and sustain your business growth. Figure 9.2 shows your responsibilities as an entrepreneur.

Figure 9.2. Responsibilities of a Personal Brand Entrepreneur	
Role	**Tasks**
Chief Executive Officer (CEO)	• You are in charge of yourself and your company, which makes you the CEO. • At the end of the day, personal failure or success lies in your hands. • You make the final decision as to which company you want to start. • You are the decision maker in every aspect of life. • As the decision maker, you can choose your own destiny—and that is empowerment.
Chief People Officer (CPO)	• Whom you surround yourself with represents who you are. As the CPO, you must recruit and retain powerful allies. • You need to meet people who have shared interests but also have skills that complement your own. For instance, if you are a talented musician, then you need to connect with a business expert to further your career. • The more people you can recruit to be part of your network, the better equipped your business will be to succeed. Think about it, we are all in human resources (HR) because we have to locate and befriend people to have a social life and professional network. • The hardest part is finding the right people and giving them the right compensation and benefits so you can have a substantial business advantage.
Chief Information Officer (CIO)	• As CIO, you need to know how to create a website to share your brand with the world. If you don't, you are placing your brand at a severe disadvantage.

Chief Information Officer (CIO), continued	• You need to be able to pay attention to your industry (area of interest) and follow it. Follow the trends and do research on a continuous basis to stay abreast of the competition.
Chief Financial Officer (CFO)	• Everyone in the world has to be her own CFO, because at some point in our lives, we will be accumulating wealth. Don't solely rely on financial advisors; start learning how to control and invest your money. • Consider all options for using your resources to establish and promote your brand and make wise, cost-effective decisions. • Utilize the strength of your network for financial advice and planning. Whenever possible, ask the experts you know.
Chief Marketing Officer (CMO)	• A CMO typically owns the PR arm of a business as well. As your own "personal PR" person, you need to represent yourself at all times. • You are the key spokesperson for your personal and corporate brand. Everything you say and do can be used for or against you. • You need to put on your marketing hat and never take it off. Every new person you meet can change your life, so have your best marketing pitch ready. • Learn about online marketing, direct marketing, public relations, and advertising—this knowledge will only play in your favor.

Getting Started

Financing Your Business

Starting your own business is a challenging but rewarding process. One of the biggest challenges any new business venture faces is securing the necessary funding to get it off the ground. It really depends on the nature of the business and the start-up costs. For instance, if you want to start your own restaurant, you will have to pay for food, labor, rent, management, maintenance, insurance… and the list goes on. If you start a Web company, your time might be the only expense (at first), but don't underestimate the value of your time.

Some entrepreneurs fund their own companies, while others seek investors, such as venture capitalists. Venture capitalists are individuals who invest in companies they believe will be highly profitable; a venture capitalist's goal is to get a maximum return on investment (ROI). Unless you have the financial backing to make your new business your full-time endeavor, you might want to start it on the side. When it grows, then you can decide if you want to do it full-time.

Here are a few obstacles you may endure:

- Acquiring all the necessary tools, materials, and inventory
- Being young, having no credit, and asking for a loan from the bank
- Finding a place to rent, getting financing, and doing interior decorating
- Paying taxes for your business while still sorting out student loans
- Having little experience and success while proving yourself to investors

Leveraging Social Media

The majority of small businesses take two to five years to become profitable. Companies must constantly reinvest in marketing to get the word out to a larger and larger audience. It's hard for a company to compete if no one knows about it. The good news is that social media is very inexpensive, if not free, and is a prime means of connecting with potential customers and employees alike.

Social media brings new meaning to entrepreneurship. The best way to get started is to surround yourself with other entrepreneurs, especially those who have already had business success. Communication through blogs and wikis is a way for multiple parties to conceive ideas, collaborate on business plans, and organize a brand-new company. By being straightforward and transparent online, you are welcoming people to be a part of your business.

As commander YOU, you can be *intrapreneural*, meaning that you have the ability to start your own product lines or open up new methods of communication, such as social media, within your current company.

> Welcome to the new world of entrepreneurial marketing that is being transformed by social networking, blogging, and conversion of the masses into new enterprise owners!
>
> —John L. Nesheim, entrepreneurship professor, Cornell University, and author of *High Tech Start Up*

The Role of Education

Colleges preach that moving up the corporate ladder is the standard, yet it's only one path to career success. Many schools only have one or two entrepreneurship classes. Typically it's not until graduate school that classes are built around entrepreneurship, but by then, it's too late—the most prestigious universities require students to have a few years of work experience to be admitted. This might be one reason why many of the most successful people drop out of college—for example, Ralph Lauren and Kanye West. Entrepreneurship is more tied to imagination than age or education.

❝ I wish school had prepared me to take my own ideas and desires to make the world a better place and put them into action, independently. I hate that the path leading to the job market is so well-worn but the path to an independent, more meaningful living is so obfuscated, despite being paid exorbitant lip service by those in school. ❞

—Alec Resnick, recent graduate, MIT

Having a Business Plan

Your company may be a magazine, a blog with advertising, a convenience store, or a technology start-up. Whatever it is, always develop a business plan first, paying special attention to the marketing portion. Remember that all potential investors are looking for ideas that are already successful, meaning that the business already has customers or millions of registered users or a clear, believable plan to get them. Investors want to eliminate as much risk as possible to make money.

Entrepreneurship is about seeing an opportunity and capitalizing on it by drafting and executing a plan. Whether you're sitting in a parking garage, standing in an elevator, or lying in bed, ideas may come to you. What separates commanders from infantry is actually following through with ideas and bringing dreams into reality.

Discover a problem that is affecting a large group of people. Once you know the "pain point," brainstorm what products might soothe that pain, so you can provide a solution. If you're situated within an organization, then be critical of how processes impact the bottom line, as well as what markets your company isn't serving. These are all opportunities where you can make a difference.

Even if you're helping out the company for which you work, instead of your own company, you are strengthening your brand and developing more achievements to include in your tool kit.

There are so many opportunities out there! You will find these opportunities by networking with other people, who can help you accomplish your business goals. Successful entrepreneurs are determined, passionate, and action oriented. They have heart and an inborn desire to make a difference, both in their own life and that of others. Entrepreneurs aren't going out every night partying till 4:00 AM. Instead, they sacrifice part of their social life as a trade-off to starting, growing, and maintaining their business ventures. Successful entrepreneurs find, connect, and befriend other successful entrepreneurs, sharing ideas and possibly becoming partners.

Do you have what it takes to be the next successful entrepreneur?

Chapter 10
Life-Changing Results

A man who was once a confused college graduate, struggling to find his place in the world and eager to make his career goals a reality, was able to discover the power of his personal brand and take command of his life. As you probably guessed, I'm speaking of myself. Personal branding has become a way of life for me. Every day, I remind myself the following: "This is my brand, and I'm passionate about it. Nothing will get in my way as I find success. Quitting is not an option—my future is too important."

If you, too, are serious and passionate about making your successful future a reality, then wait no longer! Today is the day to get started. Discover your best personal brand—including the traits that make you special and the skills that make you a unique and valuable commodity—and show the world that you are ready to seize control of your life, make your mark on the world, and achieve all of your goals. There is no better time to get started than right now.

1 2 31 2 3 41 2 3 4 5

Conquer the Obstacles

There was a point in my life when I was unfocused, lethargic, disappointed about my lack of progress, and tired of feeling that each day was the same. I had feelings of depression and anxiety over my current position. I felt trapped in my job and was nearing the point where I wanted to leave the company and pursue other opportunities. No matter how hard I worked and how outstanding my management was, it just wasn't for me any longer.

When I discovered what I wanted to do with the rest of my life, I quickly realized that my current position wasn't aligned to my brand development plan any longer. I enjoyed leaving the workday behind and blogging, podcasting, and working on building my personal brand and wanted to focus on this effort.

> The effect of personal branding on Dan is quite astonishing.... What struck me was the speed at which Dan was able to build a reputation in personal branding outside of work that eventually made its way into his professional life and opened up opportunities and doors that would never have been possible using traditional methods.
>
> —Jason Mundy, director, EMC

The journey has not been easy, but the rewards have certainly been worth the effort. All of my hard work and dedication to developing and promoting my personal brand came to a head in 2007; an article was published in *Fast Company* entitled "The Young Turks of Personal Branding," which highlighted all of my current achievements.

The article first spoke about how Tim Ferris, the famous author of the best-selling book *The 4-Hour Workweek*, branded himself for success. It then pointed out that he was an old man compared to me (I was 23 at the time). I was called "a personal branding force of nature," and all of my current achievements were covered: my TV show, magazine, blog, awards, and bylined articles. There was no hiding after that! I was on my way to achieving all of my goals.

There was a time in my life when all of the negative feelings I was experiencing could have squashed my dreams and kept me from getting to where I am today. But I refused to look at these negatives as insurmountable obstacles. Instead, I looked at them as minor hurdles, easily jumpable if I had the strength and courage to confront them head-on. Recognize that you are not alone; everyone experiences self-doubt and fear. Do not let these emotions overwhelm you—recognize them, confront them with all the tools I've given you in this book, and conquer them!

The Perks of Personal Branding

It's hard to argue with the notion that celebrities get lots of perks. Thanks to their personal brand appeal (as evidenced by armies of loyal fans eager to support them), famous actors, musicians, and others are targeted by some of the world's leading brands. From high-end designer clothing to jewelry, electronics, cars, and more, these brands are willing to give up lots of expensive freebies in an effort to get celebs to associate themselves with them. Such high-powered endorsements can really help grab audiences and profits.

Much like Hollywood celebrities, other people with recognized brands can reap the benefits. You too can be a brand celebrity! You might not appear on TV or have thousands of screaming fans waiting for you to walk down the red carpet, but people do know about you. You can be famous in a particular field or area in which you excel. When people discover your talents and you really stand out from the crowd (remember *differentiation?*), you, too, can have your own fan base. With effective online and offline branding, you can inch closer to superstardom every day!

After building my brand by following the four-step process outlined in this book, I became a leading resource in the personal branding industry. I was recognized as an expert in the field and attracted media attention from both traditional and new sources, such as Yahoo! Finance, *The Boston Globe*, ABC News, *Business Week*, and dozens of other websites, books, and magazines. My work was published in *BrandWeek* and *Advertising Age*, and my name was really getting out there. I was gaining a serious reputation and respect for my work and brand at the ripe old age of 24. After *FastCompany* wrote about my Personal Branding journey, a vice president from my company recruited me to be the first social media specialist, without even applying for it!

Before long, people were coming to me for advice. A world of corporate and personal branding consultancy opportunities opened up to me. When my blog became the leading source of information for personal branding online, I was able to interview celebrities, including Philip Rosedale (founder of Second Life), Robert McGovern (founder of CareerBuilder), Matt Mullenweg (founder of WordPress), Gina Bianchini (founder of Ning), Marshall Goldsmith, John Kotter, and Marcus Buckingham.

> **Social media has brought with it a complete disruption of traditional communications channels. What that means to the average person is that you no longer need to be a media baron or movie star or business mogul to get your name out there.**
>
> **—Maggie Fox, partner, The Social Media Group**

After countless contributions to other blogs, websites, and magazines, my branded media outlets became a vehicle for others interested in building their own brands.

Authors started sending me their books for review before they went into print. Hundreds of respectable websites started linking to my blog, magazine, and personal brand website. My subscription base soared. Before long, my blog was ranked among the top career blogs, job blogs, and marketing and media blogs by *Advertising Age*.

> **Blogging allowed me to start the conference LeWeb3, gathering now 1,300 people from 40 countries in Paris, without any marketing, just because that community enjoys meeting each other. I have no idea how I could have done that without blogging and social software.**
>
> —Loic Le Meur, serial entrepreneur and founder, Seesmic.com

Once your brand starts taking off, use this momentum to your advantage. When colleges started becoming aware of me, I started holding workshops with their students, training them on how to discover and create their own brands in preparation for graduation. I even received an invitation from Google to be an inaugural speaker for its newly established Marketing Talks@Google, and accepted a position on the board of advisors for a new geo-social networking site entitled "((echo))MyPlace."

This is just the beginning for me. My hard work and dedication to growing and promoting my brand will ensure that my future is full of wonderful opportunities for success. And I want *your* future to be just as bright!

When people chase after you and are interested in what you have to say and offer, you, too, can become a brand celebrity. It's never been easier to make this happen than now; the power of the Internet and the social media tools available to you can open a universe of new opportunities and help you achieve brand recognition at lightning speed. All it takes is for you to get serious and get started!

Meet Some Brand Commanders

I'm not the only one who has used my strategies for creating a powerful personal brand and found success. Lots of eager young individuals have proven that with the right combination of skill, determination, networking, and timing, you can transform yourself into a brand superstar. The following success stories depict individuals who realized the potential of new media and pursued their passions.

Brand Commanders Ryan Healy and Ryan Pough

- **Who:** Millennials who have gone from bloggers to CEOs in a year
- **Ages:** 24
- **College:** Pennsylvania State University, 2006 graduates

Ryan and Ryan 1.0:

- Ryan H. and Ryan P. were roommates in college, bound together by their views, enthusiasm, and knowledge of the millennial generation.
- After college, Ryan H. was a financial consultant at IBM in Washington, D.C., but was eager for more.
- Ryan P. was a freelance writer for a variety of newspapers in New Jersey and held a position in corporate communications at Merck & Company. He wanted to expand his career horizons and find true career fulfillment.

Ryan and Ryan 2.0:

- They developed Employee Evolution (*employeeevolution.com*), a blog community devoted to expressing the concerns and opinions of young people entering the workforce. It had over 1,700 dedicated Millennial contributors and readers.
- Their site was featured in the *Boston Globe*, *New York Times*, and *Wall Street Journal* and on *60 Minutes*.

- Ryan H. and Ryan P. have been branded as two of the top millennial-generation experts on the Internet.
- Because of their reputation and visibility, a well-known blogger and columnist for the *Boston Globe* decided to join forces with them in the creation of a new company, entitled Brazen Careerist.

Lessons learned:

- As a result of their success, Ryan H. and Ryan P. learned the importance of exploiting their passions and surrounding themselves with like-minded people.
- You must focus on network building and find mentors who already have strong media connections to expand and be successful.

Brand Commander Sarah Austin

- **Who:** College radio show host who became a successful online celebrity video producer
- **Age:** 21
- **College:** Washington State University, set to graduate in 2010

Sarah 1.0:

- Sarah was a tech news producer at KALX 90.7 when she first became interested in online TV.
- Before YouTube, she watched online shows like *Rocketboom*, *MoBuzz*, and *StoryToday*.
- Sarah wanted to turn her interests in online TV into a successful venture.

Sarah 2.0:

- She was part of D7tv with her video show called *Party Crashers*, where she videotaped her attempts at crashing parties, including the Yahoo! and Google Christmas parties.

- She launched *Pop17.com*, a podcast focused on how technology has changed our lives and allowed for greater personal empowerment.
- Sarah allows viewers to interact with her live during her weekly show.
- She also covers tech events, such as Macworld and CES.
- Her show is now sponsored by TechCrunch, Perkett PR, and Virgin America Airlines.
- She has interviewed Robert Scoble, Jeff Jarvis, Richard Branson, MC Hammer, Leonardo DiCaprio, Orlando Bloom, Steve Jurvetson, and Steve Wozniak.
- She's been seen on CNBC, CBS news, CityTV, and ABC News.

Lessons learned:

- It's not easy to manage being a full-time entrepreneur while still attending college, but if that's your passion, it's worth the effort.
- Make and keep a schedule/calendar that you use religiously. This way, you can commit to balancing your time and life effectively. Lifestyle organization will make you healthier and help you to get things done.

Brand Commander James Kotecki

- **Who:** Amateur video commentator turned noted expert political spokesperson
- **Age:** 23
- **College:** Georgetown University, 2007 graduate

James 1.0:

- James was always into domestic politics, even though he majored in international politics in college.

- James was eager to blend his passion for politics with his belief that candidates should be using video podcasts and YouTube for their campaigns.

James 2.0:

- James started creating a series of politically themed podcasts, using a simple webcam and Windows Movie Maker.
- His first podcast series can be seen at *ca.youtube.com/EmergencyCheese*.
- He conducted his podcasts in his college dorm room, where he mimicked mainstream news broadcasts and then transitioned to giving unsolicited advice to political candidates.
- Due to the relevancy of his content to the 2008 presidential campaign and the uniqueness of his niche, he was featured on the YouTube homepage.
- *The Economist* named James "probably the world's foremost expert on YouTube videos posted by presidential candidates."
- James has been cited in the *Los Angeles Times* and the *Washington Post* and on CNN, *The Montel Williams Show*, and Fox News to name a few.
- He hosted Congressman Ron Paul in the first-ever dorm room interview with a presidential candidate.
- He now directs his new podcast series, *PlaybookTV*, for Politico.com.
- James is also on the advisory board of Declare Yourself 2008.

Lessons learned:

- Always be accessible to your audience; keep in touch with them and maintain positive and productive conversations.

- To make it big on YouTube, be entertaining and keep it short. Jim Cramer, host of *Mad Money*, may not always be right in his stock picks, but people watch him because he is amusing.

Take these success stories to heart; learn from these eager young go-getters and realize that they are no different from you. By mobilizing your brand and positioning it for success, you are capable of accomplishing amazing things.

Start Today!

If you've learned nothing else from this book, understand that your personal brand has as much potential for success as any company. You need to have confidence in your own abilities—or no one else will. Give value to others without asking for anything in return and support your network as much as you can. Harvest your brand both online and offline and make it shine for your target audience.

Please don't be afraid to be yourself—craft your brand wisely and be authentic and natural as you communicate it to others. And never forget: there are no insurmountable obstacles if you are determined and focused enough and put in the necessary effort and investment into your successful future.

Don't live your life in the passenger's seat. Take command of your life—be commander YOU! As you progress in your career, take advantage of the amazing tools available for developing and promoting your brand—including blogging, podcasting, social networks, and whatever technological wonders are just around the corner. Imagining success in your life requires no start-up costs, and there are no good excuses for not getting started today on developing your goal achievement action plan. Today is the day you need to take ownership of your future. It's your time to make a difference.

You, too, can be a personal brand success story. The next time you look at a mirror, imagine Me 2.0—and make it happen!

Acknowledgments

I'm very thankful to everyone who has helped me along the way as I've pursued my passion for personal branding. These include people who have gone out of their way to lend a hand, who have supported my activities, or have helped make this book and my dreams possible. My parents have made great efforts in raising me, keeping faith in me, and acknowledging my work. It might have been impossible to write this book, in combination with a full-time job and all of my other projects, without my friends and family. I appreciate your kindness, sympathize with your frustrations, and applaud your graciousness through the best and worst of times.

My family, including my mom, dad, uncles, and grandparents, were indispensable when I was writing this book. I would also like to note a few extraordinary people who stood beside me through the years—I am blessed to have you close.

My closest friends, including Jonathan Mitman, Tim Hare, Angela Sanchioni, Carly Milden, and Nick Vaccaro have been invaluable assets as I've pursued my passion.

Jeffrey Adams, Jason Alba, Alexia Anaya, William Arruda, Joel Bachaler, Marc Baron, Jeff Bender, Connie Bensen, Ryan Benevides, Scott Bradley, Jeremy Buchman, Bob Carp, Raymond Chan, Robert DeAngelis, Jonathan Dioli, Alison Doyle, Andrew Dumais, Jessica Dunham, Maria Elena Duron, Chloe Finklestein, Donna Fontenot, Geoff Gates, Paul Gillin, Simon Green, Jordan Heller, Brandon Huebner, David Juengst, Fallon Katz, Guy Kawasaki, Katryn McGaughey, Kevin Kempskie, Vikram Killampalli, Debbie Lalone, Meghan Liu, Joe Markey, Wendy Marx, Brian Mason, Rick Mahn, Selina McCusker, Brian McGrath, Drew McLellan, Nogen Melamed, Corey Merrill, Edward Meyer, Tiffany Monhollon, Caitlin Mooney, Jason Mundy, Dylan Oteri, Justin Orkin, Sarah Parrish, Stephen Pazyra, Bob Percheski, Robert Pfeiffer, Amanda Pluta, Samir Popat, Robert Quinn, Brandon Reiser, Nicole Riel, Jason Ryan, Adam Salamon, Angela Sanchioni, Rebecca Thorman, Rachel Tuhro, Jenn Wilson, Russell Wyner, Kevin Vacca, Matt Vaillancourt, Liz Yurkevicz

As you learn, grow, and excel in your career, always acknowledge the support that got you there. When you become successful, help your close friends find success as well, because in the end, they are who matter most. You are only as strong as your network, and true happiness only exists with the people who surround your life.

Personal Branding Glossary

4 Ps of personal branding—Person, place, price, and promotion

Action plan—A plan that contains several line items with the title of the task, the time frame in which the task must be accomplished, and the cost

AdSense—Google's contextual advertising solution for website owners

Advertising—A paid approach to delivering a message to an audience by methods such as television or radio

Appearance—A combination of your dress, behavior, and body language

Audience—How you measure personal branding success; whom you connect and communicate with

Audience analysis—Researching and discovering the people who reflect your brand and would be interested in it

Authenticity—Who you are and what you can deliver

Avatar—A picture, 128 × 128 pixels in size, which can be used on your blog and throughout social networks

Baby boomers—Those born between 1946 and 1964, now in their 40s up to traditional retirement age

Backtype.com—Traces every blog where someone comments about you.

Blog—An online diary written in chronological format

Blogger relations—The rules of engagement when communicating with bloggers

Blogroll—A listing of favorite websites or blogs

Blogosphere—The entire body of blogs on the Internet

Brand creation—Development of personal marketing content that is delivered through online and offline means

Brand discovery—Determining your brand and creating a plan to develop its value

Branding—Creating an image for a product, service, organization, or person that resonates with the attitudes, behaviors, and perceptions of the target market.

Budgeting—Creating an itemized list of income and expenses with records that include a description, the amount of the transaction, and the date

Bylined articles—Articles written for the purpose of promoting your brand in various media sources

Career life coach—A resource that helps people learn about career and job options by giving them advice, either through consultancy or within institutions

Chicklet—A small graphic that acts as pathway to a blog's feed or posts from that blog

Commander—An individual who has the confidence, mental strength, stamina, and posture to confront the recruitment process

Competitive analysis—Assessment of the people who are providing the same product or service as you

Corporate brand—A corporate brand name used to promote a product or service

Credibility—A measure of your comprehension of a particular field or practice

Del.icio.us—A tool to bookmark, organize, and share websites

Differentiation—A distinct quality or attribute that separates one person from the next

Digg—A social network that allows you to submit and rate news, with the goal of news about you reaching Digg's homepage

Employer branding—Providing an online experience to potential candidates, employees, and other stakeholders with the goal of positively reinforcing the corporate image

Entrepreneurship—Starts one's own business with accountability and liability for the inherent risks and rewards

Evangelists—Proactive individuals who carry the message of a company or person to others

Facebook—The dominant social network that gives you free access to a variety of internally built networks, groups, and profile pages from around the world

FeedBlitz—An email subscription service for blogs

FeedBurner.com—A website that allows you to publicize, analyze, and monetize your blog subscription base

Feed reader—A tool that allows you to subscribe to and continuously view a blog

Flickr—A website that allows you to upload, tag, organize, and share all of your digital photos

FriendFeed—A site that aggregates all your social media activities

Gen X—The demographic cohort born roughly between 1965 and 1981, which tends to be cynical of institutions and focused on achieving work-life balance; more tech-savvy on average than the baby boomers but did not grow up with the Internet like Gen Y

Gen Y—The demographic cohort born roughly between 1982 and 2001, which tends to value authenticity and personal expression and be technology-proficient, demanding of their workplace, and determined to create value in their lives

Google AdWords—An advertising system built by Google that delivers targeted impressions

Google Blogger—Google's blog-hosting service

Human resources (HR)—The business function that deals with employee benefits, hiring, compensation, and promotions

Image management—Conscious manipulation of one's persona to fit a specific mold or audience

Intrapreneurial—Having the ability to start product lines or open up new methods of communication within a company

LinkedIn—A website built to facilitate professional connections that acts as a virtual resume and dynamic database for your network

Link love—Linking to other blogs for the purpose of building community

Livecasting—Broadcasting your life with video on a branded website

Market—A grouping of individuals who share similar qualities

Marketability—What makes you compelling to your audience

Marketing—Creating a transaction between a buyer and seller using promotion, advertising, public relations, direct marketing, and other methods to target a select market

Marketing strategy—A strategic plan, taking into account the

4Ps, for reaching your intended audience

Me 1.0—When people hid their corporate and personal brands, using their corporate logos as a shield.

Me 2.0—When people stand proudly beside their effective brand, regardless of ones current position or goals.

Mentor—A supportive person who lends time to help another achieve personal or professional goals

Mission statement—Your personal value statement (what you offer) and a succinct description of how your audience can benefit by choosing your personal brand

MyBlogLog—A social network that lets users display widgets on their websites with avatars of recent visitors

MySpace—Social networking platform that hosts a large installed base and allows you to create custom profile pages

Natural search—A search that lists sites higher based on links, content, and overall superiority in Google

Network strength pyramid—A diagram of the relative positions and values of various connections that you can make as you go about making your career goals a reality

Networking—The art of making connections through conversation, both online and offline

Ning—A website that allows you to launch, invite people to, and facilitate your own social network in minutes

Octopus model of relevancy—A diagram in which the head of the octopus is you and each tentacle represents an area that either impacts or is influenced by your brand

PageRank™—A search algorithm developed by Larry Page and Sergey Brin of Google that ranks sites based on links and other elements

Paid search—A way to give advertisers the ability to purchase key words so their ads show up on the front page of search results for those words

Pbwiki—One of the most popular wiki services

Perception—A quick and intuitive awareness of situations based on sensations, which can be used as the basis for decisions

Persistence—An inherent desire to achieve a specific goal, no matter what it takes

Personal brand development plan—A strategic framework that guides how you share your brand with the world

Personal brand statement—A single sentence that covers your areas of skill and mastery and who your target audience is

Personal branding—The process by which individuals and entrepreneurs differentiate themselves and stand out from a crowd by identifying and articulating their unique value proposition, whether professional or personal, and then leveraging it across platforms with a consistent message and image to achieve a specific goal

Personal branding toolkit—A set of materials that can be leveraged for each part of the recruiting cycle and beyond

Personal e-brand—A digital representation of you on the Internet

Personal marketing plan—A strategic way for you to utilize your personal development plans toward achieving your career goals

Personal PR—An individual becoming his or her own PR person or spokesperson

Personal press kit—A compilation of elements that illustrate your brand, such as description of experience, a bio, and testimonials; can be distributed to the media or used to solicit speaking opportunities

Personal press release—A document or Web page that contains a personal story, encompassing links, multimedia, and sharing capabilities

Personal SWOT analysis—Individuals need to maximize their strengths, reduce weaknesses, identify opportunities, and stabilize threats

Personal value statement—What you stand for

Personality—Your ability to communicate and interact with all sorts of people, including your peers and colleagues

Podcast—A short, user-generated video with optional sharing capabilities

Product brand—An object you can hold or see that is tied to a corporate brand

Public relations (PR)—Maintaining relationships with the media to advance and protect your brand

References document—A list of your top professional contacts

Reputation—An expectation of delivery

Reputation management—The act of ensuring your brand's accuracy, legitimacy, and relevancy over its life cycle

RSS—"Really simple syndication"; tool that allows users to view content (feeds) from other websites in one area

Search engine optimization (SEO)—The process of using search engines to increase the relevant traffic for a given website

Second Life—A virtual world inhabited by avatars created by participants who congregate online

Situational analysis—Examines where you currently are in life (current situation), as well as your short- and long-term goals

SlideShare—A social network for sharing Microsoft PowerPoint presentations

Social media—Content that enables community participation

Social networking—An online form of networking that takes place through user interaction

Sphere of influence—An imaginary area encompassing you and the individuals who have endorsed you and your personal brand

StumbleUpon—A service you can use to discover and share content from any site on the Internet and make recommendations to the rest of the network

Tag cloud—A widget that displays a group of key words with the most tagged phrase in the largest font and the least tagged in the smallest font

Technorati—A blog search engine and link-tracking website

Transparency—The ability to be seen through so that you come across as authentic

Twitter—A microblogging service where you can create an account, send short messages, and follow your friends' accounts to receive their updates

Upcoming.org—A social network that allows you to store, explore, and share events

Value proposition—What your brand stands for, including your appearance, personality, and skills

Value statement—What is true to you or what gives your brand meaning

Values—What is true to you or what gives your brand meaning

Viddler—A video-sharing website, much like YouTube but allowing for longer videos

Video resume—A video of you performing a self-interview

Video resumes—Short video clips (< three minutes) in which candidates give a summary of their credentials and positive attributes

Virtual world—A computer-based simulation of reality

Vision statement—Describes what your brand is destined to be, if you put in the work

Web 1.0—Stationary Web pages with little interactivity and only one-way communication

Web 2.0—Environments on the Web reflecting the transition from one-way communication to community-driven interaction

Widgets—Applications stored on the sidebar(s) of your blog (the areas that remain constant as you scroll down each blog entry)

Wiki—A website that enables collaboration through real-time editing without coding knowledge

Word-of-mouth (WOM)—A marketing approach by which you create buzz about your brand so others talk about it and its reputation spreads

WordPress—The zenith of blog-hosting services

YouTube—A website owned by Google that allows anyone with a video camera to broadcast his or her brand

Endnotes

1 "70% of Gen Y Leave First Job within Two Years." *Experience Inc*, September, 4, 2008.

2 Brent, Paul. "Gen Y workers start labour revolution." *Workopolis*, May 7, 2008.

3 Vitak, Jessic. "Digital Footprints: Online identity management and search in the age of transparency." Pew Internet & American Life Project, www.pewInternet.org/PPF/r/229/report_display.asp.

4 Peters, Tom. "The Brand Called You." *Fast Company*, August, 1997, pp.83.

Chapter 1

5 Dan Schawbel & Experts. "The Real Definition of Personal Branding." personalbrandingwiki.pbwiki.com.

6 Thompson, Clive. "The See-Through CEO." Wired Magazine, March, 2007, Issue 15.04.

7 Keller Fay Group. "Keller Fay's Talktrack™ Reveals Consumer Word of Mouth." www.kellerfay.com/news/TalkTrack5-15-06.pdf.

8 Thomas, Owen. "Bank intern busted by Facebook." *Valleywag*, November 12, 2007.

9 Tucker, Eric. "Web networking photos come back to bite defendants." *Associated Press*, July 19, 2008.

10 Scoble, Robert. "Meet the Press." Fast Company Magazine, April 2008, Issue 124.

[11] Scheetz, L. Patrick. "Recruiting Trends, 1997-98: A National Study of Job Market Trends for New College Graduates among 477 Businesses, Industries, and Governmental Agencies." Education Resources Information Center, no. ED461321.

[12] Tapscott, Don. "Wikinomics: How Mass Collaboration Changes Everything." New York: Penguin Portfolio, 2006.

[13] Friesen, Wes. "Maximizing your most important asset – your people." *BNET*, February 2001.

[14] eMarketer. "Now US is Online, And How!" Article. www.emarketer.com/Article.aspx?id=1005984&src=article1_newsltr.

[15] Peter, Tom A. "College grads face tougher job market." *The Christian Science Monitor*, May 5, 2008.

[16] CollegeGrad.com. "Survey Results Detail What Top Entry Level Employers Want Most." Press release. www.collegegrad.com/press/what-employers-want.shtml.

[17] Careerbuilder.com "Slower, but Steady Hiring Expected for the New Year, CareerBuilder.com's Annual Job Forecast Reveals." http://careerbuilder.com/share/aboutus/pressreleases-detail.aspx?id=pr409&sd=12/26/2007&ed=12/31/2008.

[18] "MonsterTRAK's Annual Entry-Level Job Survey Reveals an Improved Job Market for 2007 Graduates." Monster Worldwide, Inc, http://phx.corporate-ir.net/phoenix.zhtml?c=131001&p=irol-newsArticle&ID=980665&highlig.

[19] eMarketer. "Blogs and Traditional Media." The Bivings Group, http://emarketer.com/Article.aspx?id=1006327.

[20] Wikipedia Entry. "Blog." Wikipedia.org, http://en.wikipedia.org/wiki/Blog.

[21] David Sifry, Report on "The State of the Live Web, "Sifry's Alerts Blog, report posted April 5, 2007, www.sifry.com/alerts/archives/000493.html.

[22] eMarketer. "The Blogosphere: A Mass Movement from Grass Roots." Article. http:// emarketer.com/Report.aspx?code=emarketer_2000494.

Chapter 2

[23] Banjo, Shelly. "A Perfect Match?" *The Wall Street Journal*, October 23, 2008.

[24] Fortune Staff. "100 Best Companies To Work For." *Fortune Magazine*, February 4, 2008.

[25] Technorati. "State of the Blogosphere 2008." http://technorati.com/blogging/state-of-the-blogosphere.

Chapter 4

[26] Mary Rownd, comment on "The New Definition of Marketing," AMA Blog, comment posted January 22, 2008, http://appserver.marketingpower.com/blog/amablog/2008/01/the_american_marketing_associa.html.

[27] Wikipedia Entry. "Corporate Branding." Wikipedia.org, http://en.wikipedia.org/wiki/Blog.

[28] Donald Trump, comment on "The Trump Brand," The Trump Blog, comment posted February 21, 2006, http://www.trumpuniversity.com/blog/index.cfm?blogpost_id=791.

- Endnotes -

[29] Helm, Burt. "2008 BusinessWeek/Interbrand Best Global Brands Ranking." *BusinessWeek Magazine*, September 18, 2008.

[30] MacDonald, Patrick. "Weezer: A breath of fresh, fun air." *The Seattle Times,* October 10, 2008.

[31] MarketingSherpa. "Viral Hall of Fame 2008." Pink for the Cure, http:/marketingsherpa.com/viralawards2008/3.html.

[32] Vitak, Jessic. "Digital Footprints: Online identity management and search in the age of transparency." Pew Internet & American Life Project, www.pewInternet.org/PPF/r/229/report_display.asp.

[33] Starner, Tom. "Creative Recruiting on the Rise." *Human Resource Executive*, March 5, 2008.

[34] ClearSwift. "Internet and Web 2.0 Creates Unfamiliar Battleground for HR Professionals." Press release. www.clearswift.com/news/item.aspx?ID=1351.

[35] Vault Research Report. "89% of Employers Open to Viewing Video Resumes: Vault Video Resume Survey." Vault.com, www.vault.com/video-resume.

[36] Bruce, Chaddus. "CIA Gets in Your Face(book)." *Wired*, January 24, 2007, Tech Biz Section.

[37] Technorati. "State of the Blogosphere 2008." http://technorati.com/blogging/state-of-the-blogosphere.

[38] Johnson, Jerry. "Reporters Survey on Journalism, Social Media and the Blogosphere." *BRODEUR*, January 2008, Presentation.

[39] Sapieha, Chad. "Your Google reputation could cost you a job." *Globe and Mail*, January 25, 2008.

[40] CareerBuilder.com. "One-in-Five Employers Use Social Networking Sites to Research Job Candidates, CareerBuilder Survey Finds." http://sev.prnewswire.com/workforce-management/20080910/AQW02510092008-1.html.

[41] Sapieha, Chad. "Your Google reputation could cost you a job." *Globe and Mail,* January 25, 2008.

[42] Second Life. "Economic Statistics." Secondlife.com, http://secondlife.com/whatis/economy_stats.php, August 14, 2008.

[43] Jana, Reena. "American Apparel's Virtual Clothes." *BusinessWeek*, June 27, 2006.

[44] Simone Brunozzi, comment on "How I got hired by Amazon.com," Simone Brunozzi Blog, comment posted May 22, 2008, http:// brunozzi.com/en/2008/05/22/how-i-got-hired-by-amazoncom.

[45] Lawson, Stephen. "Second Life creates a millionaire." *IT World*, November 30, 2006.

[46] "Gartner says 80 Percent of Active Internet Users Will Have A "Second Life" in the Virtual World by the End of 2011." Gartner, www.gartner.com/it/page.jsp?id=503861.

[47] "89% of Employers Open to Viewing Video Resumes: Vault Video Resume Survey." Vault.com, www.vault.com/video-resume.

[48] Deloitte Consulting LLP. "Competing for Talent." Deloitte, www.deloitte.com/dtt/cda/doc/content/us_tmt_CompetingForTalent_030608FINAL%281%29.pdf, March 7, 2008.

[49] Rigoli, Elaine. "Sodexho Says Second Life Job Fairs Caters Up Quality Candidates." *Ere.net*, May 22, 2007.

[50] Bradford, Stacy L. "Experts Offer Their Tips For Fruitful Networking." *Wall Street Journal*, February 28, 2005.

[51] Carlin, Dan. "Corporate Wikis Go Viral." *BusinessWeek*, March 12, 2007.

[52] BusinessWeek Staff. "The Water Cooler Is Now On The Web." *BusinessWeek*, October 1, 2007.

[53] "U.S. Internet Users Viewed 10 Billion Videos Online in Record-Breaking Month of December, According to comScore Video Metrix" comScore, http://comscore.com/press/release.asp?press=2051.

[54] Fallows, Deborah. "Almost half of all Internet users now use search engines on a typical day." Pew Internet & American Life Project, www.pewInternet.org/pdfs/PIP_Search_Aug08.pdf.

[55] "Visual attention to Online Search Engine Results." De Vos & Jansen and Checkit, http://checkit.nl/pdf/eyetracking_research.pdf.

[56] SBA. "Frequently Asked Questions." Sba.gov, http://www.sba.gov/advo/stats/sbfaq.txt (accessed April 6, 2008).

Chapter 5

[57] Birmingham City Council. "Dress for Success." Birmingham.gov.uk.

[58] Godin, Seth. "Purple Cow: Transform Your Business by Being Remarkable." New York: Penguin Portfolio, 2003.

Chapter 6

[59] Beshara, Tony. "Part 1: Working with Recruiters." Word Bloom, http://workbloom.com/recruiting/working-with-recruiters.aspx.

[60] "GenX2Z College Brand Study." Anderson Analytics, http:// marketingcharts.com/television/college-students-love-their-brands-2080.

[61] Williamson, Debra Aho. "Social Network Marketing: Ad Spending and Usage." eMarketer, December 2007, www.emarketer.com/Reports/All/Emarketer_2000478.aspx?src=report1_home.

[62] eMarketer. "Mobile Social Network Growth Ahead." Article. www.emarketer.com/Article.aspx?id=1005982&src=article2_newsltr.

Chapter 7

[63] Nielsen/NetRatings. "Month of December 2007, Panel Type: Home." Global Index Chart, www.nielsen-netratings.com/resources.jsp?section=pr_netv&nav=1.

[64] eMarkter. "Radio Trends: On Air and Online." Report Summary, www.emarketer.com/Report.aspx?code=emarketer_2000409&src=report_summary_reportsell.

[65] Perez-Pena, Richard. "More Readers Trading Newspapers for Web Sites." *New York Times*, November 6, 2007, Advertising Section.

[66] eMarketer. "Online Video: Seeing the Whole Picture." Article, www.emarketer.com/Article.aspx?id=1005256.

[67] BuckHollywood.com. "About Michael Buckley." Michael Buckley, http://buckhollywood.com/about.

[68] Navarro, Mireya. "Love Him or (He Prefers) Hate Him." *New York Times*, July 29, 2007.

[69] Johnson, Jerry. "Reporters Survey on Journalism, Social Media and the Blogosphere." *BRODEUR*, January 2008, Presentation.

Chapter 8

[70] CSIA. "CSIA Compilation of Data Sources for Information on Cyber Security Issues." CSIA Data Compilation, www.csialliance.org/resource/csiadatacompilation.

[71] Gantz, John F. "The Diverse and Exploding Digital Universe." *IDC*, March 11, 2008, IDC Whitepaper Sponsored by EMC.

[72] Techweb Media. "Offline Website Promotion. Examples of Guerilla Marketing." Sergey Rusak. www.techwebmedia.com/2008/01/14/offline-website-promotion-examples-of-guerilla-marketing.

[73] MacMillion, Douglas and Walters, Helen. "Guerilla Marketing Gone Wild." *BusinessWeek*, February 9, 2007.

Index

- Index -

About the Author

Dan Schawbel is the leading personal branding expert for Gen Y. *Fast Company* calls Dan a "personal branding force of nature."

Dan has introduced a whole new generation to personal branding, as he opens up new opportunities and strives to elevate the practice. His Personal Branding Blog is consistently ranked in the top 100 marketing blogs in the world by *Advertising Age* and has achieved syndication by *Forbes*, *Reuters*, and the *Chicago Sun Times*. Dan publishes *Personal Branding Magazine*, is the head judge for the Personal Brand Awards, and directs Personal Branding TV.

He has written articles for major magazines and online resources, such as *BrandWeek*, *PRWeek*, About.com, Web Worker Daily, *T+D*, *Small Business Opportunities*, MarketingProfs, *Advertising Age*, TheLadders.com, and the American Marketing

Association. He is a frequent media commentator, cited in such outlets as *Fast Company, Business Week, Entreprenuer,* ABC News, Boston.com, Monster.com, *Young Money,* BNET, ReadWriteWeb, *Providence Business News, Marketing News, Brand Strategy* (UK), and Yahoo! Finance. Dan coauthored *Age of Conversation 2: Why They Don't Get It?* in 2008.

Dan has eight years of marketing experience at companies such as EMC, Reebok, Lycos, LoJack, and TechTarget. He is on the board of advisors for a geo-social network company called ((Echo))MyPlace. Also, Dan is keynote speaker at colleges and universities and helps individuals and companies with branding. He was invited to be one of the inaugural marketing speakers at Google. Dan graduated magna cum laude from Bentley College (now Bentley University), Waltham, Massachusetts, in 2006.